BROOKLANDS BOOKS

MUSCLECAR & HI-PO ENGINES
CHEVY
350 & 400

A book in The Hot Rod Magazine
' Great American Engines ' series.

ISBN 1 85520 0961

Published by
Brooklands Books Ltd., PO Box 146, Cobham, Surrey KT11 1LG, England
Printed in Hong Kong

BROOKLANDS BOOKS

BROOKLANDS ROAD TEST SERIES
AC Ace & Aceca 1953-1983
Alfa Romeo Alfasud 1972-1984
Alfa Romeo Alfetta Coupes GT. GTV. GTV6 1974-1987
Alfa Romeo Giulia Berlinas 1962-1976
Alfa Romeo Giulia Coupes 1963-1976
Alfa Romeo Giulietta Gold Portfolio 1954-1965
Alfa Romeo Spider 1966-1990
Allard Gold Portfolio 1937-1958
Alvis Gold Portfolio 1919-1967
American Motors Muscle Cars 1966-1970
Armstrong Siddeley Gold Portfolio 1945-1960
Aston Martin Gold Portfolio 1972-1985
Austin Seven 1922-1982
Austin A30 & A35 1951-1962
Austin Healey 100 & 100/6 Gold Portfolio 1952-1959
Austin Healey 3000 Gold Portfolio 1959-1967
Austin Healey Sprite 1958-1971
Avanti 1962-1983
BMW Six Cylinder Coupes 1969-1975
BMW 1600 Col. 1 1966-1981
BMW 2002 1968-1976
Buick Automobiles 1947-1960
Buick Muscle Cars 1965-1970
Buick Riviera 1963-1978
Cadillac Automobiles 1949-1959
Cadillac Automobiles 1960-1969
Cadillac Eldorado 1967-1978
High Performance Capris Gold Portfolio 1969-1987
Chevrolet Camaro SS & Z28 1966-1973
Chevrolet Camaro & Z-28 1973-1981
High Performance Camaros 1982-1988
Camaro Muscle Cars 1966-1972
Chevrolet 1955-1957
Chevrolet Corvair 1959-1969
Chevrolet Impala & SS 1958-1971
Chevrolet Muscle Cars 1966-1971
Chevelle and SS 1964-1972
Chevy Blazer 1969-1981
Chevy EL Camino & SS 1959-1987
Chevy II Nova & SS 1962-1973
Chrysler 300 1955-1970
Citroen Traction Avant Gold Portfolio 1934-1957
Citroen DS & ID 1955-1975
Citroen SM 1970-1975
Citroen 2CV 1949-1988
Shelby Cobra Gold Portfolio 1962-1969
Cobras and Cobra Replicas Gold Portfolio 1962-1989
Cobras & Replicas 1962-1983
Chevrolet Corvette Gold Portfolio 1953 1962
Corvette Stingray Gold Portfolio 1963-1967
High Performance Corvettes 1983-1989
Daimler SP250 Sport & V-8250 Saloon Gold Portfolio 1959-196
Datsun 240Z 1970-1973
Datsun 280Z & ZX 1975-1983
De Tomaso Collection No.1 1962-1981
Dodge Charger 1966-1974
Dodge Muscle Cars 1967-1970
Excalibur Collection No.1 1952-1981
Facel Vega 1954-1964
Ferrari Cars 1946-1956
Ferrari Dino 1965-1974
Ferrari Dino 308 1974-1979
Ferrari 308 & Mondial 1980-1984
Ferrari Collection No.1 1960-1970
Fiat-Bertone X1/9 1973-1988
Fiat Pininfarina 124 + 2000 Spider 1968-1985
Ford Automobiles 1949-1959
Ford Bronco 1966-1977
Ford Bronco 1978-1988
Ford Consul. Zephyr Zodiac MkI & II 1950-1962
Ford Cortina 1600E & GT 1967-1970
Ford Fairlane 1955-1970
Ford Falcon 1960-1970
Ford GT40 Gold Portfolio 1964-1987
Ford RS Escorts 1968-1980
Ford Zephyr Zodiac Executive MkIII & MkIV 1962-1971
High Performance Escorts Mk1 1968-1974
High Performance Escorts Mk II 1975-1980
High Performance Escorts 1980-1985
High Performance Escorts 1985-1990
High Performance Capris Gold Portfolio 1969-1987
High Performance Mustangs 1982-1988
Holden 1948-1962
Honda CRX 1983-1987
Hudson & Railton 1936-1940
Jaguar and SS Gold Portfolio 1931-1951
Jaguar XK120 XK140 XK150 Gold Portfolio 1948-1960
Jaguar MkVII VIII IX X 420 Gold Portfolio 1950-1970
Jaguar Cars 1961-1964
Jaguar Mk2 1959-1969
Jaguar E-Type Gold Portfolio 1961-1971
Jaguar E-Type 1966-1971
Jaguar E-Type V-12 1971-1975
Jaguar XJ12 XJ5.3 V12 Gold Portfolio 1972-1990
Jaguar XJ6 Series II 1973-1979
Jaguar XJ6 Series III 1979-1986
Jaguar XJS Gold Portfolio 1975-1990
Jeep CJ5 & CJ6 1960-1976
Jeep CJ5 & CJ7 1976-1986
Jensen Cars 1946-1967
Jensen Cars 1967-1979
Jensen Interceptor Gold Portfolio 1966-1986
Jensen Healey 1972-1976
Lamborghini Cars 1964-1970
Lamborghini Countach Col No.1 1971-1982
Lamborghini Countach & Urraco 1974-1980
Lamborghini Countach & Jalpa 1980-1985
Lancia Stratos 1972-1985
Land Rover Series I 1948-1958
Land Rover Series II & IIa 1958-1971
Land Rover Series III 1971-1985
Land Rover 90 & 110 1983-1989
Lincoln Gold Portfolio 1949-1960
Lincoln Continental 1961-1969
Lotus and Caterham Seven Gold Portfolio 1957-1989
Lotus Cortina Gold Portfolio 1963-1970
Lotus Elan Gold Portfolio 1962-1974
Lotus Elan Collection No.2 1963-1972
Lotus Elite 1957-1964
Lotus Elite & Eclat 1974-1982
Lotus Turbo Esprit 1980-1986
Lotus Europa Collection No.1 1966-1974
Marcos Cars 1960-1988
Maserati 1965-1970
Maserati 1970-1975
Mazda RX-7 Collection No.1 1978-1981

Mercedes 190 & 300SL 1954-1963
Mercedes 230/250/280SL 1963-1971
Mercedes Benz SLs & SLCs Gold Portfolio 1971-1989
Mercedes Bens Cars 1949-1954
Mercedes Bens Cars 1954-1957
Mercedes Bens Cars 1957-1961
Mercedes Bens Competion Cars 1950-1957
Mercury Muscle Cars 1966-1971
Metropolitan 1954-1962
MG TC 1945-1949
MG TD 1949-1953
MG TF 1953-1955
MG Cars 1959-1962
MGA & Twin Cam Gold Portfolio 1955-1962
MGB MGC & V8 Gold Portfolio 1962-1980
MGB Roadsters 1962-1980
MGB GT 1965-1980
MG Midget 1961-1980
Mini Cooper Gold Portfolio 1961-1971
Mini Moke 1964-1989
Mini Muscle Cars 1961-1979
Mopar Muscle Cars 1964-1967
Morgan Three-Wheeler Gold Portfolio 1910-1952
Morgan Cars 1960-1970
Morgan Cars Gold Portfolio 1968-1989
Morris Minor Collection No.1
Mustang Muscle Cars 1967-1971
Oldsmobile Automobiles 1955-1963
Old's Cutlass & 4-4-2 1964-1972
Oldsmobile Muscle Cars 1964-1971
Oldsmobile Toronado 1966-1978
Opel GT 1968-1973
Packard Gold Portfolio 1946-1958
Pantera Gold Portfolio 1970-1989
Plymouth Barracuda 1964-1974
Plymouth Muscle Cars 1966-1971
Pontiac Tempest & GTO 1961-1965
Pontiac Firebird and Trans-Am 1973-1981
High Performance Firebirds 1982-1988
Pontiac Fiero 1984-1988
Pontiac Muscle Cars 1966-1972
Porsche 356 in the 60's
Porsche Cars in the 60's
Porsche Cars 1960-1964
Porsche Cars 1964-1968
Porsche Cars 1968-1972
Porsche Cars 1972-1975
Porsche Turbo Collection No.1 1975-1980
Porsche 911 1965-1969
Porsche 911 1970-1972
Porsche 911 1973-1977
Porsche 911 Carrera 1973-1977
Porsche 911 Turbo 1975-1984
Porsche 911 SC 1978-1983
Porsche 914 Gold Portfolio 1969-1976
Porsche 914 Collection No.1 1969-1983
Porsche 924 Gold Portfolio 1975-1988
Porsche 928 1977-1989
Porsche 944 1981-1985
Range Rover Gold Portfolio 1970-1988
Reliant Scimitar 1964-1986
Riley 11/2 & 21/2 Litre Gold Portfolio 1945-1955
Rolls Royce Silver Cloud 1955-1965
Rolls Royce Silver Shadow 1965-1981
Rover P4 1949-1959
Rover P4 1955-1964
Rover 3 & 3.5 Litre Gold Portfolio 1958-1973
Rover 2000 + 2200 1963-1977
Rover 3500 1968-1977
Rover 3500 & Vitesse 1976-1986
Saab Sonett Collection No.1 1966-1974
Saab Turbo 1976-1983
Shelby Mustang Muscle Cars 1965-1970
Stubebaker Gold Portfolio 1947-1966
Stubebaker Hawks & Larks 1956-1963
Sunbeam Tiger & Alpine Gold Portfolio 1959-1967
Thunderbird 1955-1957
Thunderbird 1958-1963
Thunderbird 1964-1976
Toyota Land Cruiser 1956-1984
Toyota MR2 1984-1988
Triumph 2000. 2.5. 2500 1963-1977
Triumph GT6 1966-1974
Triumph Spitfire Gold Portfolio 1962-1980
Triumph Stag 1970-1980
Triumph Stag Collection No.1 1970-1984
Triumph TR2 & TR3 1952-60
Triumph TR4-TR5-TR250 1961-1968
Triumph TR6 1969-1976
Triumph TR7 & TR8 1975-1982
Triumph Herald 1959-1971
Triumph Vitesse 1962-1971
TVR Gold Portfolio 1959-1990
VW Beetle Collection No.1 1970-1982
VW Golf GTi 1976-1986
VW Karmann Ghia 1955-1982
VW Kubelwagen 1940-1975
VW Scirocco 1974-1981
VW Bus. Camper. Van 1954-1967
VW Bus. Camper. Van 1968-1979
VW Bus. Camper. Van 1979-1989
Volvo 120 1956-1970
Volvo 1800 1960-1973

BROOKLANDS ROAD & TRACK SERIES
Road & Track on Alfa Romeo 1949-1963
Road & Track on Alfa Romeo 1964-1970
Road & Track on Alfa Romeo 1971-1976
Road & Track on Alfa Romeo 1977-1989
Road & Track on Aston Martin 1962-1990
Road & Track on Auburn Cord and Duesenburg 1952-1984
Road & Track on Audi & Auto Union 1952-1980
Road & Track on Audi 1980-1986
Road & Track on Austin Healey 1953-1970
Road & Track on BMW Cars 1966-1974
Road & Track on BMW Cars 1975-1978
Road & Track on BMW Cars 1979-1983
Road & Track on Cobra, Shelby & GT40 1962-1983
Road & Track on Corvette 1953-1967
Road & Track on Corvette 1968-1982
Road & Track on Corvette 1982-1986
Road & Track on Datsun Z 1970-1983
Road & Track on Ferrari 1950-1968
Road & Track on Ferrari 1968-1974
Road & Track on Ferrari 1975-1981

Road & Track on Ferrari 1981-1984
Road & Track on Fiat Sports Cars 1968-1987
Road & Track on Jaguar 1950-1960
Road & Track on Jaguar 1961-1968
Road & Track on Jaguar 1968-1974
Road & Track on Jaguar 1974-1982
Road & Track on Jaguar 1983-1989
Road & Track on Lamborghini 1964-1985
Road & Track on Lotus 1972-1981
Road & Track on Maserati 1952-1974
Road & Track on Maserati 1975-1983
Road & Track on Mazda RX7 1978-1986
Road & Track on Mercedes 1952-1962
Road & Track on Mercedes 1963-1970
Road & Track on Mercedes 1971-1979
Road & Track on Mercedes 1980-1987
Road & Track on MG Sports Cars 1949-1961
Road & Track on MG Sprots Cars 1962-1980
Road & Track on Mustang 1964-1977
Road & Track on Nissan 300-ZX & Turbo 1984-1989
Road & Track on Peugeot 1955-1986
Road & Track on Pontiac 1960-1983
Road & Track on Porsche 1961-1967
Road & Track on Porsche 1968-1971
Road & Track on Porsche 1972-1975
Road & Track on Porsche 1975-1978
Road & Track on Porsche 1979-1982
Road & Track on Porsche 1982-1985
Road & Track on Porsche 1985-1988
Road & Track on Rolls Royce & B'ley 1950-1965
Road & Track on Rolls Royce & B'ley 1966-1984
Road & Track on Saab 1955-1985
Road & Track on Toyota Sports & GT Cars 1966-1984
Road & Track on Triumph Sports Cars 1953-1967
Road & Track on Triumph Sports Cars 1967-1974
Road & Track on Triumph Sports Cars 1974-1982
Road & Track on Volkswagen 1951-1968
Road & Track on Volkswagen 1968-1978
Road & Track on Volkswagen 1978-1985
Road & Track on Volvo 1957-1974
Road & Track on Volvo 1975-1985
Road & Track - Henry Manney at Large and Abroad

BROOKLANDS CAR AND DRIVER SERIES
Car and Driver on BMW 1955-1977
Car and Driver on BMW 1977-1985
Car and Driver on Cobra, Shelby & Ford GT 40 1963-1984
Car and Driver on Corvette 1956-1967
Car and Driver on Corvette 1968-1977
Car and Driver on Corvette 1978-1982
Car and Driver on Corvette 1983-1988
Car and Driver on Datsun Z 1600 & 2000 1966-1984
Car and Driver on Ferrari 1955-1962
Car and Driver on Ferrari 1963-1975
Car and Driver on Ferrari 1976-1983
Car and Driver on Mopar 1956-1967
Car and Driver on Mopar 1968-1975
Car and Driver on Mustang 1964-1972
Car and Driver on Pontiac 1961-1975
Car and Driver on Porsche 1955-1962
Car and Driver on Porsche 1963-1970
Car and Driver on Porsche 1970-1976
Car and Driver on Porsche 1977-1981
Car and Driver on Porsche 1982-1986
Car and Driver on Saab 1956-1985
Car and Driver on Volvo 1955-1986

BROOKLANDS PRACTICAL CLASSICS SERIES
PC on Austin A40 Restoration
PC on Land Rover Restoration
PC on Metalworking in Restoration
PC on Midget/Sprite Restoration
PC on Mini Cooper Restoration
PC on MGB Restoration
PC on Morris Minor Restoration
PC on Sunbeam Rapier Restoration
PC on Triumph Herald/Vitesse
PC on Triumph Spitfire Restoration
PC on VW Beetle Restoration
PC on 1930s Car Restoration

BROOKLANDS HOT ROD 'MUSCLECAR & HI-PO ENGINE SERIES
Chevy 265 & 283
Chevy 302 & 327
Chevy 348 & 409
Chevy 350 & 400
Chevy 396 & 427
Chevy 454 thru 512
Chrysler Hemi
Chrysler 273, 318, 340 & 360
Chrysler 361, 383, 400, 413, 426, 440
Ford 289, 302, Boss 302 & 351W
Ford 351C & Boss 351
Ford Big Block

BROOKLANDS MILITARY VEHICLES SERIES
Allied Mil. Vehicles No.1 1942-1945
Allied Mil. Vehicles No.2 1941-1946
Dodge Mil. Vehicles Col. 1 1940-1945
Military Jeeps 1941-1945
Off Road Jeeps 1944-1971
Hail to the Jeep
US Military Vehicles 1941-1945
US Army Military Vehicles WW2-TM9-2800

BROOKLANDS HOT ROD RESTORATION SERIES
Auto Restoration Tips & Techniques
Basic Bodywork Tips & Techniques
Basic Painting Tips & Techniques
Camaro Restoration Tips & Techniques
Chevrolet High Performance Tips & Techniques
Chevy-GMC Pickup Repair
Custom Painting Tips & Techniques
Engine Swapping Tips & Techniques
Ford Pickup Repair
How to Build a Street Rod
Mustang Restoration Tips & Techniques
Performance Tuning - Chevrolets of the '60s
Performance Tuning - Ford of the '60s
Performance Tuning - Mopars of the '60s
Performance Tuning - Pontiacs of the '60s

CONTENTS

INTRODUCTION

Hot Rod Magazine has from its inception in January '48 been performance orientated. The key to high performance is the engine, and Hot Rod's editors have for over forty years kept their readers' interest by commissioning articles on how to maintain, tune, repair, restore and modify the popular power plants of the period.

If ever there was a golden age for American engines it must be from the mid 50s when the small block Chevy made its debut to the early 70s when emission controls brought an end to the musclecar era. The three major manufacturers. GM, Ford & Chrysler each supported at least one big block and one small block engine during this period which subsequently went on to become automotive legends.

This book is one in our Hot Rod on Great American Engines series. Its purpose is to bring together a comprehensive selection of the best and most informative stories on one or one family of engines. It is targeted at todays younger enthusiasts with a view to letting them know what was written about their power units during this exciting period. If older readers enjoy a nostalgic trip through these pages, so be it.

The stories included here have been drawn from Hot Rod and Car Craft magazines and from other Petersen publications of the period. We are, as always, indebted to the Petersen Publishing Company for allowing us to re-issue these copyright technical articles in this way. Our thanks also go to Lee Kelley and John Dianna for their personal help and support over the years.

R.M. Clarke

DISTRIBUTED BY

Brooklands Books Ltd., PO Box 146, Cobham, Surrey KT11 1LG, England
Phone 0932 865051. Fax 0932 868803

Brooklands Books Ltd., 1/81 Darley St., PO Box 199, Mona Vale, NSW 2103,
Australia. Phone 2 997 8428.   Fax 2 416 7996

Motorbooks International, Osceola, Wisconsin 54020, U.S.A.
Phone 715 294 3345. Fax 715 294 4448

PROJECT CAMARO

by Jim McFarland

The 350-cubic-inch engine is the latest (along with the 302) variant in what's been happening over the last dozen years to the engine that Chevrolet dropped on the public in 1955. Like its forebears, the 350 is amenable to all sorts of major and minor operations, only about 23 cubic inches more so. The editors of *HOT ROD,* as always, were eager to find out just what this newest offering liked or did not like in the way of deviations from "box stock." The test bed chosen was a straightforward Camaro 350 SS and, just to keep things interesting, a 396 engine was ordered as a side dish to go in the hole when the 350 was being operated on.

Our object was to bring the engine up to blueprint specifications, provide it with a few street-worthy performance parts, and see just how well the results would compare with the numbers derived from the 396-incher. Bob Joehnck (of Santa Barbara, California) got the nod as both assembler and consultant; a direct consequence of the many and current successes he has been having with the smaller Stovebolts. (To wit, one of the projects of late has been a steel/glass Camaro capable of running high 10's and 130-plus with a single three-barrel carburetor sitting over only 350 cubic inches!) So here are the steps involved in revamping the stock engine.

Following initial teardown, the complete works was soused in the hot-tank. Cam bearings were knocked from the block, as were the small core plugs that you'll find at the perimeter of the block's rear camshaft plug. Removal of these is the *only* trick by which the block can be properly flushed; a "must" move if honing and/or boring cuts are to be made. Just tap and plug these holes with Allen-headed stoppers whenever the cleanup work is finished.

Next, the block was align-bored; an operation we ought to spend a couple of lines discussing with you. Contemporary Chevy engines frequently come supplied (from the factory) with both undersize and tapered bearings. This is a design feature intended to compensate for production variations in bore alignment and a condition which should be corrected if you plan even semi-serious performance work with the finished product. So align-bore the block and replace all the mains and rod inserts with standard-sized parts. In addition to a balance job, have the crank checked for trueness (be sure it's straight!) and do a little polishing on the bearing surfaces. Building to a clearance of .0025-.003 for main bearings and .0025 on the rods should bring everything up to snuff in the bearing department. Factory recommended torque loadings will suffice (70 ft. lbs. on the mains, 30-32 ft. lbs. on the rods). Rod side clearance was increased to .010-inch per pair of rods (accomplished by the removal of .0025-inch from *each side* of each rod).

Next, although the small-block Chevy likes piston clearance, it was felt that use of the stock aluminum pistons would require skirt clearance to be confined to a maximum of .003-inch (measured just below the oil ring groove and at right angles to the piston pin). Since these are autothermic units, you should consider .003 as a reasonable limit for street engines. For piston rings, a Ramco moly-filled top ring, a chrome faced second ring (take your pick among the ring makers) and a double steel rail chrome oil ring worked as the best combination used.

Ring end-gap "mumbo-jumbo" can get pretty confusing at times, so you can use the following as a rule of thumb: Allow a minimum of .004-inch of end gap for each inch of cylinder bore diameter (for top rings only . . . the others will take care of themselves). Other clearances should be checked pretty closely as you assemble the engine, since dimensional stackups can sometimes throw things pretty far out of kilter.

Cam bearings were replaced, too. Unless you knock these out of the block before the cleaning operations begin, you'll never rid the grooves behind the cam bushings of the grit that collects during metal cutting. We just wanted to report that. Bob prefers Federal Mogul solid steel-backed cam bearings, so these went into place prior to cam location.

The oil pump remained basically stock, but the free length of the oil relief spring was increased ⅛- to ¼-inch. You can just stretch it a little; not too many people will complain. All the square corners in the pump's passages were smoother (radiused), the pickup tube was brazed into position

A small (but happy) happening with a Chev 350

1

2

3

(locate the pickup so that it just clears the pan's bottom), and the pickup screen by-pass hole was soldered up. The stock 350 pan was used, and of course the oil pump was the customary hi-perf small block Chevy unit that's been around for a number of years (part 3848908).

The heads got the customary Joehnck treatment (write him if you'd like the same); a mild valve pocket cut, a little trim in the intake side of the combustion chamber, a .020-inch slice from the head to true the surface and to compensate for the small amount of metal removed from the chambers (static ratio was held at the stock 10.5:1), and a set of PC Teflon and rubber valve seals. Valve springs supplied in the Racer Brown cam and kit package used (cam SSH-44, 292-degrees duration, .510-inch net lift) required a mild spot-facing of the spring seats. With this accomplished, the springs were a "twist fit" into their

seats and over the seals. Spring pressure is about 95-100 pounds with the valves seated.

Racer's ability to produce an extended rpm hydraulic 'shaft were apparent when the engine was accidentally nudged to the rpm limiter's automatic cutoff of 7000! It would appear his insistence that rpm ceiling for "soft lifter" cams is a function of lobe profile is not without foundation. Remember the Power-Pack '56 Chevy hydraulic 'shaft that pumped the lifters at 5300? Progress.

With this particular camshaft, the valve pockets in the pistons required a bit of touching up. All you need do is select the pocket of least depth, slip a slice of clay over the pockets (both intake *and* exhaust), install a head, a used gasket and enough valve gear to operate the valves attending the cylinder under investigation, and rotate the crank through a *complete* firing cycle. Re-

move the head, check the valve-depressed thickness of the clay and allow a minimum clearance of .090-inch. If the valve notch requires a slight trim job, a discarded valve with notches cut in its perimeter, installed through a guide (with the head on the block) and in the end of an electric drill, will make a fine shade-tree valve notch reliever.

One note regarding modification (or the lack of it) to the stock valves: Don't remove the swirl polish on the backside of the valve head. The finish is designed to help dissipate valve head heat. It took GM considerable time and money to develop this little refinement, so leave it and the misty finish on the top of the valve head as they are. You can, however, replace the stock 350 exhaust valving with units (part 3849818) from hi-perf 327 heads if you decide the price of a pair of these high-squeeze, good-breathing lids are beyond the capabilities of your pocketbook.

Stock steel shim head gaskets were

1. Virtually ready to drop in the car, the project Camaro 350 bristles with good things like Hooker headers, Mallory Rev-Pol igniter. Strong stuff.

2. Topping off the engine is an Edelbrock C3B high-rise manifold and the 3916-A Holley three-barrel carb.

3. Holley was modified with a new kit from Edelbrock to cure flat spot. Air cleaner is replaceable element Hellings.

4. Stock heads were surfaced, a must to remove any unevennesses and low spots.

5. Valve openings were unshrouded and the throats carefully blended by reaming followed by careful grinding.

6. Intake ports were opened slightly, smoothed and straightened. Polishing is necessary.

7. Parallel surface grinding is a good idea on any block to assure 90-degree bore angle and true surfacing.

used but you could just as well use one of the conventional pack-type designs if that's what you already have. Head installation (at least using the Joehnck method) isn't as per the usual approach. First, Bob uses hardened steel washers under each head bolt and brings the engine setup to the first 50 ft. lbs. with three torquing steps. From this point on up to the final load of 70 ft. lbs., he just works his way through the pattern in steps of about two ft. lbs. It takes a little time, but Bob claims gasket and thread life will be much improved.

One point you really should consider is the use of a thrust button in the nose of the camshaft. Unfortunately, much camshaft wear can be attributed to the front-to-back movement of the 'shaft during normal engine operation. So unless you use the sintered iron crank gear (not the old-style heat-treated one), the late type nylon timing gear (the narrow version) and an aluminum plug placed in the cam sprocket, you are running the risk of trouble, particularly if the engine is equipped with stiff valve springing and a performance camshaft. Bob has a kit containing both gears (timing and crank), a new Morse chain and the aluminum button. Regardless of where you get the pieces, just make certain you do.

We finally returned to the stock distributor. Total advance was limited to 12-degrees (distributor) in at 3000 engine rpm, a set of 1966294 Delco points was installed, the vacuum advance mechanism was disconnected and overall spark lead was found to work best (with all the other equipment in use) at 42-degrees . . . a little rough for the street, but "finer than frog's hair" for the strip. With the advance plate tack-brazed to the distributor housing and the modification just mentioned (plus the "Flash-Fire" Mallory coil), the igniter was good for everything up to the self-imposed 7000 rpm engine cutoff.

On the street, plugs were AC 44's. Any number of combinations will work on the strip. We never really altered the overall weight of the car (the last weigh-in showed 3260), so the 2.56 low gear Muncie, the 4.56 rear gear and the lightweight aluminum flywheel and Rev-Lok (Schiefer) were the final combination. With this environment, the little engine seemed to like Gary Hooker's 30-inch-long, 1¾-inch-diameter, 10-inch collector headers the best, so we strapped these back on.

Problems with the Holley three-barrel were cured with a couple of quick Edelbrock-derived changes to the secondary opening system. The photo should give you an idea of what we did, and if you purchased one of these packages at some time in the past and are having flat-spot problems, check with Vic and he'll straighten it out.

1. Head should be surfaced on same machine as the block if possible to assure equal indexing and tooling.

2. Care in setting up crank pays off. Crush-fit bearings first then assemble with good lube. Crank should spin free.

3. Part of Edelbrock kit for curing Holley flat spot—secondary metering body, diaphragm cover and spring.

4. Soft plugs at the rear of the oil galleries were removed and pipe-thread allen screws fitted in their place.

5. Berry Plastiglass hood weighs 40 lbs. less than stock and provides needed air flow around carburetor.

6. Light and easily removed, nylon "blast blanket" was used for the necessary approved scattershield.

That three-barrel is some kind of a carburetor!

Performance? Thought you'd never ask. But first, you might want to know that we managed to get the car to a 13.02 before the 350 was snatched and replaced with the 396. Performance equipment at that point amounted to a rear gear (the same with which we concluded the project), a lightweight 'wheel, a set of headers (again the same unit), a high-rise manifold, a set of lift bars (still on the car), and the 350-hp Chevy hydraulic camshaft . . . 13.02. You thought we should have done a mite better, but we weren't losing any races.

This time, the numbers were a shade better: 12.52, 109. For an AHRA stocker (one carburetor and hydraulic camshaft), it's like a license to steal. You can almost eat a peanut butter sandwich between shifts and still swat the competition resoundingly.

PARTS & LIST PRICES

Racer Brown camshaft and valve train kit; SSH-44 (hydraulic series), .510-inch lift, 292-degree seat timing (duration), $85 list for the cam, $86.30 list for the hi-perf lifters, aluminum retainers and springs. With everything right, this stick is good to about 7400 rpm!

Edelbrook C3B hi-rise intake manifold and a 3916A 3-bbl Holley; $92.50 list for the manifold and $150 list for the complete carburetor. (Write Vic for the little kit he's developed to take the flat-spot out of the Holley 3-holer.)

Hellings cleanable-filter air cleaner; part number AF 800-L, $19.50 list. (This unit has been designed specifically for the 3-bbl carburetor but will work equally as well on conventional 4-bbl units.)

Berry Plastiglass fiberglass Camaro hood; specify either hinge-type or lift-off model, $112.50 list, a weight saving of about 40 pounds, and a ready way to provide much-needed air flow to the engine compartment.

Hooker headers; equal-length tubes that dump into a 3-inch collector and which can be easily installed, $125 list including all the hardware.

Hood clips from Holman-Moody; part number GT-100, $10.95 list per set of four.

Mallory "Flash-Fire" ignition coil; a universal 12-volt variable resistor unit (34-42 Kv.); part number U12A, $17 list.

Chute Metal "blanket" scattershield; a wrap-around unit that attaches to the engine's heads and covers the bellhousing, easily swapped from car to car, $90 list.

As you no doubt have noticed over the years, Detroit comes out with a new engine every so often. Then, as each succeeding model year arrives, factories beef up engines and increase displacements to gain selling points for the new model. This year, we're presented with an all-new 350 cubic inch Chevrolet engine which is actually a scaled-up version of last year's 327, giving more horsepower and better performance for the '67 model. With only two ways open to get added inches (bore and stroke), there isn't too much choice. One year they stroke, next they bore, and when they run out of material, they are faced with the problem of designing a new engine. This occurs about every 5 years or so.

When they do get something good, they are loath to discard it and are more prone to retain the proven design wherever possible. For the hot rodder, this couldn't be better because quite often the new design can be adapted to the older engine with a minimum of hassle, thereby updating the old engine.

The 350 Chevy engine's crankshaft is just such a case. Chevrolet got this engine by stroking the 327 and beefing up the rod and main bearings of the new crank and block. A comparison of the two cranks reveals just where the beefing occurs (measurements listed are in inches; include clearance for bearings):

350 Engine		327 Engine
3.480	stroke	3.250
2.100	throw	2.000
2.450	main	2.300

As you can quickly note, the stroke has been increased .230-inch, the mains have been beefed .150 and rod bearing size has been increased .100.

If you grind down the 350 crank's mains by .150-inch, the crank will drop into the 327 block. This leaves you two ways to go on the rod and piston situation. One way is to buy a complete 350 piston and rod setup and install it. The bores are the same. If your engine isn't too worn, a glaze-busting job with a hone will suffice for cylinder preparation. If the block is worn, and the bores are out of round, you're going to have to bore anyway, so you might just as well go big and get some added inches. In this case, you can use factory oversize pistons, or the special racing piston of your choice. Things will clear nicely, although a very minimal amount of grinding may be necessary where the pan flange passes the oil filter mount. Check things carefully.

The second route is to grind down both the main and rod bearings to the 327 size. Now all you need are 350 pistons; you can still use your 327 rods.

This brings up another point. If you're going to grind down the rod throws to 327 size, why not offset the grind and pick up some more stroke? Theoretically, you could grind (eccentrically) the .100 added material off the main side of the throw and gain another .100-inch of stroke. In actual practice, this won't quite work out. First, the throws aren't always indexed right on the money, and trying to grind just to the outer surface will result in a slightly flat spot at the very extreme outer face of the bearing. It is better to go for a stroke increase of .080-inch. This will result in the removal of .080-inch of material on the inner face of the throw and a .020-inch cleanup grind on the outer face of the throw.

You now have a throw that will accept the 327 rods, and a crank with 3.560 inches of stroke. By doing it this way, we have increased the 350 crank stock stroke by .080-inch. The 350 crank had a stroke increase of .230-inch over the 327 to begin with, and by offset grinding, we have added another .080-inch for a net gain over the 327 of .310-inch stroke. You now have a 358 cubic inch engine. If you punch the block out to the maximum of 4.060 inches and use the reground 3.560-inch stroke crank, you can get a total of 368.7 cubes.

Before you slap the heads on this setup, stop and think a moment. When you gained the .080-inch stroke, you raised the piston .040-inch in the bore at TDC, and lowered it the same amount at BDC to get the added .080-inch. The pistons are going to stick out of the block. Fortunately, this isn't much of a problem, as the 350 pistons have plenty of meat in the dome. Chop the top of the pistons the required .040-inch to give a zero deck height, then install two .020-inch stock factory steel shim head gaskets.

For street application with a "street-type" camshaft, piston-to-valve clearance is no problem. But when cams of racing specs enter the picture, make *sure* this clearance is checked!

This is only necessary when you go for the added .080-inch stroke by offset grinding the 350 crank's throws. The 350 stock pistons already have the pin boss holes relocated .115-inch higher to allow for the .230-inch stock stroke increase.

Remember, that piston is going .040-inch lower in the bore

at BDC with the stroked 350 crank, so turn the block over and check for piston skirt to counterweight clearance. These bigger cranks really fill the crankcase, and this could be very critical. If any material must be removed, it has to be machined off the piston pin bosses. This is a critical area, and in no case can the thickness of material between the bottom of the pin bore and the bottom of the boss be reduced to less than .190-inch. Also, the engine *must* be balanced.

When you digest one of these stories, you just don't look at the factory engineering spec sheets and speculate on what can be done. You go to someone who has done these things and has had plenty of experience with this type of operation. In this case, we made a trip downtown to CrankShaft Company and picked the brains of Hank Bechtloff, who makes a living at doing just this type of crank work. He has found out a few things that aren't quite apparent at first glance.

When Chevrolet increased the throw on the new crank, they apparently used the same forging dies that the 327 was made from. This resulted in leaving very little shoulder at the outer edges of the crank throw. CSC calls this area the thrust pad. Another thing that shows up on the new cranks is a lack of radius where the bearing surfaces meet the counterweights and throw faces. The finish in this area is rather rough, with heavy tool marks and grooves remaining after machining work. This weakens the fillet and has resulted in crank breakage. To correct this situation, CSC regrinds the bearing areas, leaving their ultra-duty radius in all the fillets. This actually strengthens the crank. Material is added by weld buildup around the outer edges of the individual crank throws to increase the torque pad area. This strengthens the crank throw, keeps the rods aligned on the throw and gives added oil control by keeping the oil from slinging out of the throw too easily. For better bearing oiling, the crank is also cross-drilled. To make a really smooth job for all-out performance, CSC adds their Ultra-rev wraparound center counterweights. After all the welding and grinding, the crank is heat-treated for stress relief. This all-out, super-keen 350 crank goes for $179.50 plus core charge.

So now all that remains to do is consult your pocketbook and decide just which way you want to go to jack that 327 up to a '67 three-fifty cubic inch hauler. ■■

Text and photos by
Eric Rickman

THE 327

Your suspicions are confirmed: the crank from Chevy's 350-incher can be made to fit the earlier small-block engines. Just follow these steps with care

```
        350" CHEV 1967 CRANK
        ALTERED TO 3.560 STROKE

Note. Std. 350" Crank Stroke is 3.480"
      Altered Crank Stroke is 3.560"

         ← 2" Dia. →
                              Moved C/L
        Orig. C/ Line          .040
                              Gained .080

                          2.100 Dia.
                          Total Stroke
```

Drawing above indicates area to be removed in eccentric grinding to gain an added .080-inch stroke when grinding the 350 crank throw down to fit the 327 rods. By this slight stroke increase, you can gain 8 cubic inches over the stock engine and still use 327 rods.

When 327 rods are used on the reground throw, block clearance is no problem (upper left). Poor finish in stock crank fillets is weak point (above right). When reground to fit 327 block, a generous fillet is retained. With eccentric grinding, or use of the 350 rods, check the pan flange clearance at the oil filter (far left). Another very critical item to watch is the piston-to-counterweight clearance at BDC. The CSC Ultra-Rev crank shown (above) has all the engineering improvements CSC has devised. Ultra-duty fillets are at all bearing radii. Crank also has cross-drilled oil passages for better lubrication. Wraparound counterweights have been added to the center main for better balance and higher revs. The thrust-pad area at the outer edge of the throws has been built up by welding (far left) for rod alignment.

11

ISKY'S WAILIN' STREET CHEVY

Twenty-two dyno-proven versions of 350 reveal a dollar/horsepower breakdown that should land a solid spot somewhere among your hop-up plans

Text and photos by Eric Rickman ■ "Horsepower costs money, how fast do you want to go?" has long been a favorite sign at speed shops. If you're still naïve enough not to believe this, just run your eye over the accompanying dynamometer charts and the list of goodies needed to get the horses.

All this came about when Ed Iskenderian decided to find out just exactly how much horsepower did cost. He called HRM and asked if we would be interested. Needless to say, this was an opportunity to gather a wealth of information to pass on to our readers. Before we go any further, let's have it understood that this isn't the only way to go; this is simply the way Ed went with his products and we are just reporting the facts.

ABOVE RIGHT—Isky's dyno man, Dave Carpenter (left), and Gen. Mgr. Norris Baronian set timing for a test run. BELOW—Stock ignition was helped with Mallory springs.

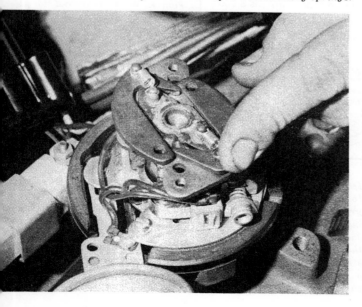

The engine Ed chose was the popular 350 cubic inch Chevrolet (the one being supplied in the Camaro and '68 Chevy II). This comes with a Quadrajet carburetor, a single-point Delco distributor and a 10:1 compression rating. Ed turned the engine over to Dave Carpenter, his dyno-room man, to prepare and run. Dave immediately tore the engine down and checked everything, in effect blueprinting the engine to be sure everything was right. Here are a few of Dave's tips: Check clearances, inspect all bearings and their oil hole alignment. Flush all lines and passages to remove shavings and core sand and deburr everything. If we can have foulups in our closely inspected Apollo spacecraft program, what makes you think Detroit checks things any closer? When you stuff that cam into your engine, the chance of keeping the engine together goes out the window unless you spend some time correcting factory oversights. It's real cheap insurance to inspect the engine before running it. To be doubly sure, Dave sent the crank to Reath Automotive (in Long Beach) and had it Polysand Micro finished. The bearing throws and mains were radiused, and the oil holes were chamfered.

The all-stock (except for the crank work) baseline run was disappointing, to say the least. GM rates the engine at 295 horses, and we were able to round up 293.7 of them. The ignition signed off at 5500 rpm, when point float was encountered. We were giving the engine a bit of an edge with a set of 1¾-inch i.d., 30-inch-long tuned headers going into 4-inch collectors and a pair of huge truck mufflers to get rid of back pressure. The ignition was given a 15-degree initial advance plus a smoother advance curve, instead of the factory-recommended 8 degrees.

Now let's look at the tests and see what we found. Since we have to settle for some orderly system, let's set up a horsepower progression chart. That's what this is all about, anyway. Test #4 gave us 4.4 horses over stock at a cost of $167.50; obviously this is no way to go. This came about as a progression from test #2, in which we gained 62.3 horses by installing a $55 cam. By the way, this was the best deal we encountered, being just over 88¢ per horse (excluding tax). Power reduction in test #3 was caused by a faulty set of ignition points. In test #4, we found that adding carbu-

(Continued on page 14)

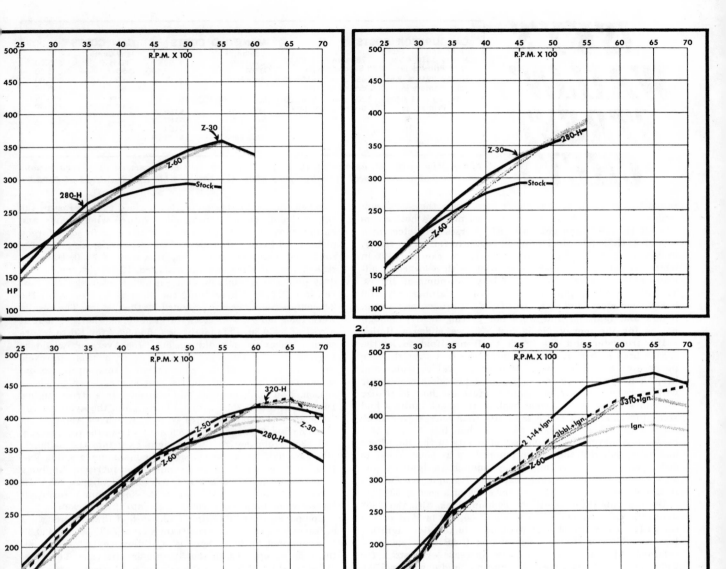

2.

4.

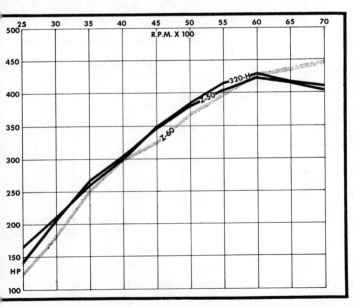

The "Z" prefix cams are run with the cam kit, the "H" cams use the Isky anti-pump-up hydraulic lifters. Graph #1 represents cam only being run in an otherwise stock engine. The 280-H is designed for a stock setup and developed 357.3 horsepower. Nothing much happened with the more radical cams. In graph #2 we replaced the Quadrajet with a 3310 Holley 4-barrel. Very little was gained because the stock ignition laid down at 55-hundred. In graph #3 we added a Roto-Faze dual-point ignition with increased dwell; now the cams are beginning to show their potential when they run on up to seven-grand. The 280-H isn't helped too much; it is a stock carb, mild cam. The Z-30, Z-50 and 320-H hydraulic come on strong. Note the power loss at the low end of the more radical Z-50 and Z-60. Graph #4 is a test of the most radical street cam Isky recommends, the Z-60. Stock, or with ignition only, nothing much happens, but when you let it breathe, it starts to come on. It got to 422.9 horsepower with a 4-barrel, jumped to 442.3 horses and was still climbing with the 3-barrel (160 more cfm of air). When we gave it 1200 cfm with 2 four-barrels on a ram log it jumped to 464.2 horses. Note the dog-leg curve up to 35-hundred where the ram effect began to work. Graph #5 represents the maximum camming and carburetion Isky recommends for street use. Note the Z-50 and the 320-H cams are almost identical.

ISKY'S WAILIN' STREET CHEVY

CARBURETOR COSTS			MANIFOLD COSTS		CAM COSTS	
Quadrajet	Stock		Edelbrock		Isky Cams	
Holley 3310 4-bbl	780 cfm	$ 80.00	C-4B	$ 92.50	280-H	$55.00
#72 Primary jet	#76 Secondary jet		C-3B	$ 92.50	Z-30	$85.00
Holley 3916-A 3-bbl	950 cfm	$150.00	X-C8 Ram	$159.50	Z-50	$95.00
#81 Primary jet	.089 drilled Secondary				Z-60	$95.00
2 Holley 1-14 4-bbls	1200 cfm	$106.00	IGNITION COSTS		320-H	$95.00
#65 Primary jet	.067 drilled Secondary		Mini Mag	$165.00	Cam Kit	$62.80
			Vertex Mag	$160.00	Anti-pump	
			Delco Trans.	$169.00	Lifters	$48.00
			Roto-Faze	$120.00		

These prices are list, as quoted at the factory. You will be surprised at the variations you can find at your local friendly speed shop. We saw a 3-bbl and manifold at $175.80.

retion to the stock engine didn't help, since the stock cam couldn't handle it. As a cross-check, we put in a hotter cam and kit (test #7) and got up to 62.1 horses over stock at a cost of $147.80 (the stock ignition began to fail at 5 grand). Following test #2 (ignition failure), we ran test #3 in which we added a Roto-Faze ignition with a locked-in advance of 44 degrees, and a set of Isky anti-pump-up lifters. This allowed the engine to reach 7 grand, gaining only 57.8 horses over stock, and at a cost of $223. Here we had a cam, lifters and ignition, and were not getting nearly enough horses for the money. So in test #5, we added a Holley 3310 carburetor and Edelbrock C-4B manifold to let the engine breathe better. Keep in mind the fact that the sole purpose of a radical cam is to open the valves wider and keep them open longer; *ergo*, you must provide a carburetor with more cubic feet per minute (cfm) air flow to realize the cam's potential. We went back to the stock ignition and stock lifters and got (with the 3310) 75.9 horses over stock for $227.50. This was about $4 more than test #3 and 18.1 horses more, even though one set of points in the Roto-Faze had collapsed. But the lifters pumped up at 5500. What to do? Spend some more money by adding an ignition and anti-pump-up lifters to bring back the 7 grand. We did this in test #6 and got 82.9 horses over stock at a cost of $395.50.

Having run through all the combinations with the 280° hydraulic cam, we moved on to the Z-30, the mildest of the solid lifter cams tested, and went back to the stock ignition for test #8. The Holley 4-barrel and C-4B manifold were retained. All this gave a 90-horse increase over stock for $320. As might be expected, the ignition "laid down" at 5500. Check this with test #6. We had more horses for less money, but we would have to spend more loot for an ignition that would keep up with the cam and carburetion. In test #9, we added the Roto-Faze (at a cost of $120), bringing the total up to $440.30. The engine developed 99.3 horses over stock and ran all the way to 7 grand.

When we got to this point, Ed decided that to insure the engine from coming apart under future wilder cams and harder runs, it would be wise to switch over to some forged pistons. Ed takes a dim view of the die-cast stock piston for continued heavy operation. So, at a cost of $350, Dave installed a set of Venolia forged, slotted, 12.8:1 pistons, heavy-duty pins and special low drag 3/64-inch-thick rings. We now ran test #10, with everything the same as #9 except for the 2.8 compression increase provided by the pistons. The results were 109.9 horses over stock (a gain of 10.6 horses), but at a cost of $930.30. This might be a fine way for Ed to insure engine longevity on the dyno, but "Joe Average" would be hurting in the financial department with this approach. Since all the rest of the runs included this setup, we did some extrapolation and got the cost figures down to within reason. You don't need all this insurance in a street engine. Disregarding the 2500 rpm 1.3-horse gain, the average gain from 3000 to 7000 computes to 8.37, which we rounded off to 8.5 horses. By subtracting 8.5 horses from the top reading, and $350 from the cost, we're right back into the ballpark, albeit about 2.1 horses low, since the maximum reading was 10.6 horses gained by the 2.8 compression increase. Applying these corrections, we get a more realistic figure of 101.4 horsepower for $540.30, only a 2.1-horse jump for $100. Horses come high when you get up into this bracket.

Comparing tests #11 and #12, we find that we get a 3.2 horsepower gain with a cost range from $435.30 to $450.30. You will notice that there is a difference in cams here: the Z-50 as opposed to the 320° hydraulic cam. The price differential is reflected in the difference between the costs of the solid lifter cam and kit with the Z-50 and the anti-pump-up lifters for the 320-H. Here, the horsepower curve must be considered when deciding which cam you need. The 320-H appears to have a bit more on the bottom-end. Remember, with more cam the engine needs to breathe better, so test #13 included a Holley 3-barrel (with an air flow of 950

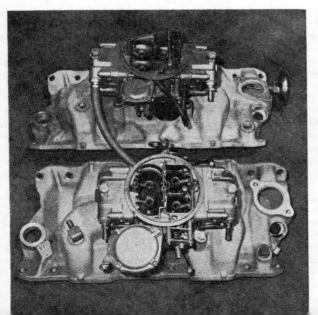

LEFT—The Holley 3310 4-barrel (top) and the Holley 3916-A 3-barrel were used on matching Edelbrock high-rise manifolds. The X-C8 Edelbrock ram log with two 1-14 four-barrels appears in lead photo (p. 48); note the Weiand air horns. These gave 9 hp on a hemi. The 3-barrel is recommended for maximum carburetion on the street. We were never able to get a cfm rating for the stock Quadrajet, but the 3310 is rated at 780 cfm, the 3316-A at 950 cfm, and the two 1-14 four-barrels will pass 1200 cfm. The cam and kit prices are Isky list and are firm.

TEST	HP INCREASE OVER STOCK	COST
#4	4.4	$172.50
#3	57.8	$223.00
#7	62.1	$147.80
#2	62.3	$ 55.00
#5	75.9	$227.50
#6	82.9	$395.50
#8	90.0	$320.00
#9	99.3	$440.30
#10	101.4	$540.30
#11	117.0	$435.50
#12	120.1	$450.30
#13	121.3	$520.30
#15	134.4	$445.30
#16	144.0	$520.30
#14	146.3	$489.30
#17	181.4	$489.30

cfm) and accompanying manifold. This gave us a corrected figure of 121.3 horsepower gain over stock for $520.30. This cam needs air, so in test #14 we gave it the works: two Holley 1-14 4-barrels on a ram manifold, with a total air flow rating of 1200 cfm. This got us a corrected gain of 146.3 horses over stock at a cost of $489.30.

Next we moved up a step to the Z-60 cam, which was a bit more radical, and went through the same carburetion steps. Test #15, with the 780 cfm 4-barrel, showed 134.4 horses over stock at a cost of $450.30. In test #16, we moved up to 950 cfm with the 3-barrel and got 144.0 horses over stock at a cost of $520.30. Test #17 was an all-out effort with an available 1200 cfm through two 4-barrels. This delivered the maximum gain of 181.4 horses over stock for $489.30. The ignition was locked at 40 degrees advance. When the lead was increased by only two more degrees, gains of 6 to 10 horses were made, indicating that radical cams are extremely sensitive to timing changes and should be power-timed for best results. Keep cranking in the lead till the power falls off, then back it off slightly.

With the cam prices being the same for the Z-50, Z-60 and 320-H, you must check the power curve closely to determine which cam is best suited to what you want it to do. Dragging requires a cam with lots of bottom- and mid-range power. For street and highway use, we would prefer a cam with plenty of mid-range. This would also be applicable for circle track racing. A top-end cam would be the ticket for the "lakes" or Bonneville. You probably noticed most of the tests were run with a Roto-Faze ignition setup. Dave ran some comparative tests between the Roto-Faze, a Mini-Mag, a Vertex magneto, and a stock Delco transistor system. The results were so close (in the stock engine) that there is really no reason for selecting any particular unit over the others, except where price is a factor. Joe Panek has a $40 lower price going for him in the Roto-Faze, so it was used in these tests to keep the buyer's budget down. While on the subject of ignitions, it should be mentioned that Dave gave the stock Delco ignition a bit of help by improving the advance curve. This was done by installing a pair of Mallory #26099 springs, an "A" and an "H." This brought the total advance to 43° (15° initial and 14° in the distributor) at 3200 and in a faster but smoother advance curve.

Obviously, if you want to gain that additional 8 to 10 horses that can be picked up with a 2.8 compression rise, you can install pop-up pistons. Simply pay your money and take your choice.

We offer this in-depth analysis with the hope that it will be of some help in guiding you in the spending of your bucks for the best deal in horsepower. ▪ ▪

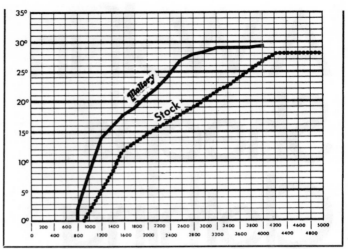

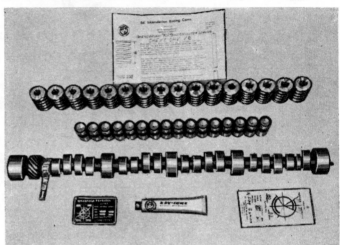

TOP — When we installed a pair of "A" and "H" Mallory #26099 springs, we were able to give the stock ignition a smoother and earlier advance curve (left). With 15 degrees initial at the crankshaft, the new setup begins to advance at 800 rpm and reaches a total of 43 degrees overall lead at 3200 rpm, instead of 4200 rpm as does the stock system. ABOVE — The kit for "Z" prefix cams has chilled iron lifters, silicon chrome springs and aluminum retainers, plus a tube of Isky's special Rev Lube, a must-use item.

Test Number	1	2	3	4	5	6	7	8	9	10	11	12	13	14	15	16	17
Carburetion	stock	stock	stock	Holley 3310	Holley 3310	Holley 3310	stock	Holley 3310	Holley 3310	Holley 3310	Holley 3310	Holley 3310	Holley 3-bbl	2 Holley 1-14	Holley 3310	Holley 3-bbl	2 Holley 1-14
Ignition	stock	stock	Roto-Faze	stock	stock	Roto-Faze	stock	stock	Roto-Faze	Mini-Mag	Roto-Faze	Roto-Faze	Roto-Faze	Roto-Faze	Roto-Faze	Roto-Faze	Roto-Faze
Cam	stock	280-H	280-H	stock	280-H	280-H	Z-30	Z-30	Z-30	Z-30	320-H	Z-50	Z-50	Z-50	Z-60	Z-60	Z-60
Manifold	stock	stock	stock	C-4B	C-4B	C-4B	stock	C-4B	C-4B	C-4B	stock	C-4B	C-3B	Edel ram	C-3B	C-3B	Edel ram
Other Accessories	none	none	Isky lifters	none	none	Isky lifters	cam kit	cam kit	cam kit	cam kit	Isky lifters	cam kit	cam kit	cam kit	cam kit	cam kit	cam kit
2500	170.8	158.7	159.0	163.4	162.8	165.6	159.3	160.7	161.2	162.5	142.5					179.2	
3000	211.5	209.8	207.1	211.7	217.0	218.3	210.3	209.3	207.1	217.35	209.0				245.7	256.7	259.9
3500	246.7	258.9	249.0	247.9	260.4	261.6	247.9	262.1	260.2	268.1	261.0	271.4	268.0		287.7	285.1	310.2
4000	273.4	288.2	280.3	273.9	298.2	299.6	284.6	296.0	297.4	305.2	299.5	310.2	302.2	323.3	287.7	285.1	310.2
4500	288.4	317.4	314.8	297.9	327.6	335.4	315.4	333.0	329.2	339.5	344.2	339.5	348.8	377.5	311.8	330.1	362.6
5000	293.7	344.5	337.4	298.1	349.7	353.3	342.4	354.0	355.8	362.2	369.2	372.1	377.8	409.2	367.4	366.8	411.8
5500	287.3	356.0	350.4		369.6	369.2	355.8	383.7	379.1	380.9	400.4	403.4	406.8	430.7	404.3	403.5	446.4
6000		332.0	351.5			376.6	331.3		388.7	400.5	418.1	421.3	422.3	448.5	415.7	440.2	471.6
6500			322.2			356.5			393.0	403.6	419.2	422.3	423.3	445.4	436.6	442.25	483.6
7000			292.9			324.9			371.7	376.7	407.7	403.5	420.2	418.4	433.5	446.2	480.0
		62.3 hp	57.8 hp	4.4 hp	75.9 hp	82.9 hp	62.1 hp	90.0 hp	99.3 hp	101.4 hp	117.0 hp	120.1 hp	121.3 hp	146.3 hp	134.3 hp	144.0 hp	181.4 hp
		$55.00	$223.00	$172.50	$227.50	$395.50	$147.80	$320.30	$440.30	$540.30	$435.50	$450.30	$520.30	$489.30	$445.30	$520.30	$489.30

To apply this information to your specific use, study the power range of each cam in relationship to the rpm range in which it is developed. Note some have lots of low-end, others low- and mid-range power, while some are strictly top-end only. Disregard test #3; we lost a point in the dual ignition. Still, there wouldn't have been enough of a gain for the cost.

A Wolf in Sheep's Clothing

Turning a small-block Chevy 350 into a sub-11-second quarter-miler is no fable . . . here's how.

By Jim McFarland

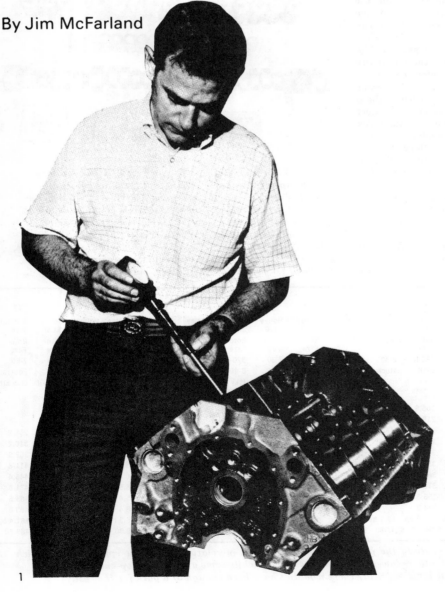

Blueprinting: "a program of action," according to Webster, and we're of the opinion Webster was way ahead of his time. Blueprinting the Chevrolet 350 is definitely a program of action — one intended to *enhance* that action on the order of darned-near doubling the stock horsepower (give or take a few horses). The "program" part is what this article is all about: the "action" we'll leave to you.

Production engines (small-block Chevys or any other kind) are just that — *production*. In order to make them available in the quantity necessary and at a price which is reasonable, mass-production techniques are required. The result is engines which perform reasonably well under ordinary driving demands placed upon them; and that is what they are intended to do. Competition applications impose a much more stringent demand on the durability and output requirements, and precision and know-how are required to produce engines capable of withstanding the demands imposed by performance applications. With this much of an explanation of the "whys" of establishing precise dimensions, clearances, balances and timing of an engine, let's get started on the above-mentioned program.

Once the engine has been completely disassembled (down to the last nut and bolt), the cylinder block main bearing holes can be align-bored. The object here is twofold: to correct any factory imperfections in saddle diameters and alignment in order to eliminate any misalignment which, under high rpm situations, could damage bearings and crankshaft; and to establish an exact reference and positioning point for machining operations which are to follow.

Because cam bores or bearings receive full oiling, have lighter loads than the crank, and have greater factory clearances — as well as the journals' being ground on centers — align-boring isn't necessary.

Cylinder decks should now be machined (by a qualified machinist — a service which is required for all machining operations set forth in this step-by-step procedure if intended results are to be achieved; otherwise, the end product may well perform as if it were constructed from badly folded blueprints!). The precisely aligned saddles produced in the previous align-boring operation will enable the machinist to position the cutting machine accurately so as to make both decks exactly at right angles to (and equidistant from) the crank centerline; to make clean, absolutely flat surfaces for seating the heads; and to set up the decks for the cylinder boring to come. A cut of .010-.012-inch is generally enough for these purposes.

Cylinder boring to obtain exact roundness and right-angle relationship to the crankshaft is next. To make sure factory imperfections are removed, yet prevent thinning of cylinder walls to the danger point, the bore should be .030 over. A block-mounted boring bar is extremely accurate and will do the job suitably — provided, of course, the user has the necessary skill. Final honing is a must for competition engines, and contrary to passenger car practices, an extra fine *wet* hone (dipped in solvent) applied in a slight cross-hatching pattern produces the best results. This fine finish is recommended for racing applications because attending modifications provide better oil supply to piston skirts, rings and upper lands, and the new rings seat quickly (without the customary break-in period). Also, emphasis in performance applications is on output rather than the passenger car engine life expectancy.

Block decks should now be grooved to accept O-rings. A cut of .030 is sufficient to enable the groove to accept the .040 diameter armature wire which will be pressed in later on.

Crankshaft oil holes should be ground to implement oil supply to the bearing stations. Generous radiusing is the way to go.

The crankshaft should now be set on centers preparatory to grinding the journals to establish bearing clearances and crankshaft trueness. The expert machinist's services are definitely called for here, but don't make the mistake of assuming the crank is true; check it carefully. The align-boring procedure performed earlier is virtually useless if the crank isn't true. For the 350 engine, clearances should be .003 for the mains and .0025 for the rod journals. A micrometer should be used to check these clearances, and the shaft's main and rod journal O.D. measurements should be compared with I.D. measurements of the respective bearing assemblies after assembly and torquing.

The next step is primarily a precautionary one — grinding the rear main cap to increase oil pump flow. A restriction exists at the oil pump which should be corrected for racing applications. With the pump hold-down bolt removed, look through the bolt passage while the pump is positioned on its main cap perch. You'll be able to detect the extent of the restriction we're talking about and see how much grinding is required.

To facilitate cleaning the block, core plugs at the front of the oil gallery should be removed and holes

2

4

3

5

tapped for ¼-inch hex pipe plugs. Opening the galleries in this way makes it possible to remove all the residue from the machining operations through thorough flushing.

The connecting rods can be reworked or replaced, depending on your budget and intended use of the engine after blueprinting. For serious competition, the forged steel rods manufactured by performance parts manufacturers or the specialized aluminum ones are recommended. The stock 350 rods are better than they used to be, but reworking is essential for high rpm conditions. Rod and/or bolt failure produces too many of the fireworks at drag facilities to be overlooked, and making sure these pieces are worthy of reconditioning via magnafluxing is the first step. The shanks should be ground and polished to eliminate tiny surface imperfections which may develop into major fracture lines under stress. Shot-peening is also recommended to strengthen rod surface areas.

1. Careful work pays off. A good engine builder checks each hole for the proper piston fit.

2. One of these holes is for the distributor, the other for a breather pipe. This is an early block.

3. Compare with photo #2. The breather hole has been eliminated in this later small-block Chevy (exact date for changeover not known).

4. Hole in rear main cap (where oil pump fits) should be cleaned out with a drill to remove all of the obstruction for greater oil flow.

5. Also, the hole in the oil pump should be cleaned out for greater flow. All oil passages should be checked for obstructions. It pays off in longer lasting bearings, and may even save your engine if you are really trompin' on it.

1

2

discussed when we get to 'em, call for a tuned exhaust system in order for the complete assembly to realize its full potential.

Four-tube collector-type headers have been proven satisfactory for the kind of Chevy we're building. They provide excellent top-end output and also supply more horsepower over a broader rpm range than other types of headers. With the cam/valve setup described in this article, headers of 1¾-inches in outside diameter should extend 30 inches from each exhaust port into 3½ O.D. collectors that are 12½ inches long. These collectors are a bit larger in O.D. than the ones often used, but they've been found to increase horsepower in the higher rpm ranges (6000 plus).

Sorry . . . we digressed. We were supposed to be talking about head modification (maybe ours could use a little). Rather than the stock 350 heads, you'll be horsepower ahead to invest in a set of 327 high-performance heads of '65-'66 vintage. They are already partially relieved in the intake areas and offer lighter weight valves with hard-chromed stems and better profiles.

The three areas receiving attention are the intake passage from the port entrance to the valve seat, the combustion chamber, and the exhaust passage from the exhaust valve seat to the port opening. Let's take them one at a time.

The port entrance on the intake passage should be ground to match the standard GM high-perf gasket opening. There's no point in enlarging the port beyond the dimensions of the gasket opening. The critical area extends from the valve guide boss to the valve seat. Incoming gas flow changes direction in the area surrounding the valve guide boss. A slight narrowing of the passage between the boss and the valve seat produces a kind of venturi effect on the flow. Maximum flow rate is reached between the opened valve and its seat. Without going into the "scientific" aspects of flow and flow modifications, keep in mind that caution should be exercised when the grinding tool is in hand. Guide wear and who-knows-what-all can result from too much enthusiasm in the head modification department. The objective is simply to even up all intake ports and blend one contour into the next.

Valve pockets on the 327 head are fully machined by the factory, and the valve head diameters are adequately large. The seats should be widened to approximately 0.100 to minimize the edge-like effect on flow of the wide valve heads. Any sharp

Full-floating type pin assemblies are easier to assemble than their press-fit counterparts. They also contribute to more even loading, are more "forgiving" of slight misalignments, and facilitate accurate alignment without danger of bending rods during the assembly process.

The machining operation involves producing rods which have exact big-end bore diameters and center-to-center distances; need we add that a professional machinist should be used?

Stock bolts and nuts should be replaced with aircraft quality forged steel counterparts or other heavy-duty pieces. Big-end distortion results when rod bolts fall down on the job, and the consequences can be disastrous. Use aluminum-bronze bushings in the small ends of rods.

With these operations completed, it's clean-up time. And this can be the most important step of all. Start with a cleaning solvent, then douse with cold water. Then scrub (really, not just hit-or-miss fashion) with hot water and detergent. Complete the operation with pressurized hot water, if possible. If cold water is all you've got, apply an extra measure of elbow

grease to each step in the sequence. This clean-up business is of vital importance, and solvent alone will *not* remove all the bits and pieces remaining from machining operations.

The next order of business concerns balancing. In an engine as carefully prepared as the one at hand, it is essential that the piston/rod/pin assembly, crankshaft, crank dampener, flywheel and clutch cover assembly, and driveshaft be completely balanced. This is another job for a specialist, but it's one that can mean the difference between success and failure of the total blueprint procedure.

Let's turn our attention now to some headwork. Improving breathing and horsepower increases go hand in hand. Head modifications to the small-block Chevy should be accompanied by attending changes in valve lift and timing and induction and exhaust systems. With these modifications, the engine will "think" it has been supercharged — more than a normal amount of that vital air/fuel mixture will be able to pass through the engine. The head modifications outlined here, together with the camshaft recommendations and intake manifolding to be edges remaining after the grinding should be removed with emery cloth. The intake valve with a polished head and swirled underside is the high-performance version, and all it needs is to have the edge beneath the lower lip ground off to produce a better radius.

The combustion chamber area around the intake valve doesn't require machining. In fact, compression can be lowered by material-removal. Small amounts of material can be removed from the very small area on the chamber wall adjacent to the intake valve's edge (spark plug side). In appearance, this area looks like a bulge close to the valve edge when the valve is fully open. This bulge is in the direct path of highest flow through the port passage, and grinding off just enough to provide more breathing room for the valve at maximum lift is the plan.

On the exhaust side of the chamber, a considerable amount of shrouding exists around the exhaust valve when it is near maximum lift. Only a *little* shrouding material can be removed because of the nearness of the edge of the head gasket, but some relief is possible. Any sharp edges or noticeable irregularities should be removed. If any milling is done, the sharp edges remaining should be chamfered by hand.

Exhaust valve seats should be widened to 0.125 to help reduce erosion of the mating surfaces and help dissipate valve head heat. The widened seat also aids in smoothing the flow of the outgoing exhaust gases.

A second venturi-type area exists in the exhaust passage, and it should be removed. Any required deburring and slight contouring to conform the passage to the exhaust gasket outline should also be done, but little if any advantages result from extensive port contouring in the exhaust area. And don't monkey around with high-performance exhaust valves; they're effective as is. The fuzzy-looking coating on exhaust valve heads is a heat-dissipating agent developed by the factory and should definitely remain on the valves.

The time has now come to start putting things back together. We can't emphasize too strongly the importance of cleanliness in assembling the engine. Everything — including you — should be subjected to a thorough cleaning prior to any installation procedures. So take time out to get tools in order and get the grease off your hands, as well as all the parts and pieces you'll be grabbing soon.

With the block completely clean and dry, how about adding a colorful touch? It's a perfect time to paint it. You know you'll have all your bud-

dies leaning over the fender after you've gotten it back together, so give them something to look at.

Use a good sealing compound such as GM 1050026 for installing the ¼-inch hex pipe plugs at the ends of the oil galleries. Slightly deburr the cam bearings' inside edges with a scraper and install the cam bearings. Put in the rear cam core plug, using some of the above-listed sealer. Install the rear main seal with Gasgacinch gasket sealer or equivalent.

Clean main bearings — even if they are brand, spankin' new — to make sure not even a trace of oil is on their backs. Coat the bearings, after laying them in place, with a good 40 weight racing oil. Lightly coat the large main cap bolt threads with oil, then torque to 70 ft.-lb. The smaller, angled bolts should be dipped in Gasgacinch (or equivalent) so that threads are heavily coated. Torque these bolts to 45 ft.-lb. The holes of these angled bolts penetrate the water jacket, so sealing is a must.

Next assemble the rod/piston/pin/ring collection you intend to install. High-compression pistons of forged, hollow-head design are very satisfactory, but you probably have your own theories about the brand you want. Just make sure they're adequate for the intended use of the completed engine. During the assembly process, use generous amounts of the racing oil on the exterior of each piston and the entire surface of each ring. Install rings with gaps alternating in positions above the pin locks. Even though rings generally have correct gap clearance when you take them out of the box, always double check. One method is to push each ring into a cylinder — using a piston as the pusher — and then measure the gap with a feeler gauge. A .004 clearance per inch of cylinder bore is a good rule of thumb, but it's better to have too wide a gap than one that's not wide enough.

Carefully clean rod bearing shells and install in the block. Before putting in the piston/rod assemblies, generously coat the rod bearings and journals with the racing oil. Then face the rod oil squirt holes toward the camshaft.

Ready for the cam? So are we. A cam such as the 66-R manufactured by Racer Brown will contribute substantially to overall enhanced performance. It has a .560-inch lift and should be installed with the special valve springs and rev kit made to accompany the 66-R cam. A new chain is recommended when installation time comes, and the aluminum-nylon-type cam sprocket is also a good investment. The cam, chain, sprockets and

3

4

1. It takes precision — and expensive — equipment to surface heads and blocks accurately. This Lempco surfacer will do the job, but a lot depends on the operator and how he sets up the head in the machine.

2. Guides much be machined to install Perfect Circle teflon valve stem seals, which means the head must be off the engine and disassembled. They really work, however, so it's worth the trouble.

3. Chamfer around head studs will prevent pull-up of metal, and the soft wire O-ring helps the head gasket to do its job effectively.

4. Most custom engine builders remove these stock soft plugs and substitute threaded pipe plugs.

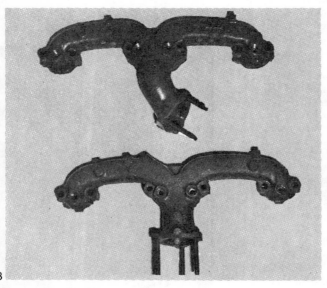

1

2

3

4

1. The only way to check ring end-gap is by putting the ring into the cylinder. On a worn cylinder, gap should be checked with the ring in the least worn part of the bore.

2. Of course you have to have grooves in the piston pin bore to use a pin lock like this. It's made in a spiral, and seems to work better than the half-circle locks that have been used for years.

3. Stock 1969 350-in. manifolds. Not bad for a stocker, but there's bound to be a lot of back pressure where the manifold branches come together at the middle.

4. Two short pieces of rubber hose should be slipped over the rod bolts before inserting the piston. It's good insurance against a bunch of scratches on a crank.

5. Stock 1969 350-in. manifold. The metal shield keeps the splashing oil from frying on the very hot exhaust heat passage.

nose thrust plug should all be coated heavily with the 40-weight oil. De-greeing the cam comes next, and a dial indicator, degree wheel and some concentration are helpful at this point. So turn off the transistor radio and focus all your attention on following the manufacturer's specifications. *Later* you may want to fool around with the timing; but start by installing to grinder's specs.

The oil pump and drive, front timing cover and pan can now be installed. Glue the pan gasket to the block with gasket cement, leaving the other gasket surface and pan edge uncoated. With this procedure, the pan can be removed as often as necessary for lower-end inspections without ruining the gasket.

Extreme care should be exercised in the next step — installing the crank dampener. With carefully balanced dampener at stake, it's smart to install it judiciously. With the dampener

degreed in 1° increments around the full circle (360°), adjustments are easier. Put the No. 1 cylinder at exact top dead center (TDC) after the dampener. With carefully balanced Mark a line with white paint on the dampener exactly even with the factory TDC zero mark. This will facilitate quick ignition timing checks.

Higher-compression engines — especially Chevys — are pretty eager to blow head gaskets. The best way to minimize this tendency is to install an O-ring in the groove made during the machining process. Tap it into place gently.

High-quality studs are recommended in place of factory cap screws in the block. They have higher tensile strength, allow more frequent head removal since they're stationary, and SAE threads permit more accuracy during torquing operations. It's best to seat these studs with teflon tape around the lower threads to prevent possible water seepage into the rocker chambers.

Thoroughly oil lifters, then install them, guide bars and the rev kit, following manufacturer's instructions on the latter. A little patience (and an extra pair of hands) is required for proper installation of the rev kit, but it'll be worth it to save that engine at super-high rpm.

Now we're ready for those reworked heads. A *good* head gasket should be purchased and lightly coated with a top quality sealer. Perma-Torque #7733 gaskets work extremely well; they compress to standard gasket thickness under torque in comparison with steel shim or composition types which tend to maintain their non-standard thicknesses after installation. They also hold the torque (although checking is advised after the first firing up).

With the heads on the block, the protruding stud threads should be oiled. Hard steel flat washers should be slipped over the studs; they'll facilitate more precise torque readings and keep the steel nuts from biting into the cast iron heads. Oil the high quality SAE nut threads and run them down against the washers. Make sure there's a good film of oil between the washers and nuts and between the threads.

Torquing is another of the critical, sometimes tedious operations which can make a lot of difference in the durability department. Torque all around at 15-pound increments until 45 ft.-lb. is reached. Now slow to 2-pound increments, following the same round and round sequence, until 60 ft.-lb. With the SAE threads being used, 60 pounds is all that's required because of greater effective pressures applied by the finer threads. The 2-pound route assures even compressing of gaskets, a must for higher rpm conditions.

Pre-oil rocker assemblies and install in place. You may want to invest in a needle bearing, roller tip-type assembly. The ball and socket in stock rocker setups are very vulnerable during racing operations because of the shorter warmup periods and spring loads, accompanying hot camshafts. You might give it some thought.

The choice of manifolding is an important one. The Edelbrock C-3B high rise with an Edelbrock-Holley 3-bbl. (#3916-A) is a proven performer on dyno tests and on drag strips. If a pure-strip charger is what you are aiming at, you may want to remove the center dividers and add a spacer to increase the size of the plenum chamber. Otherwise, simply bolt the manifold to the engine and the carburetor to the manifold. Careful at-

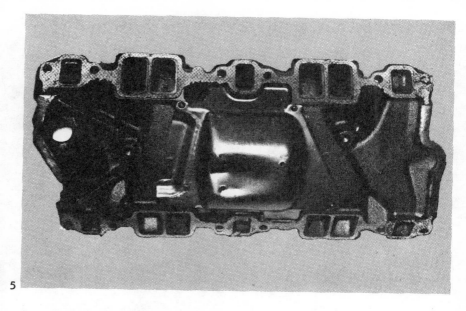

5

tention should be given to alignment and sealing of the gasket and seals. Depending on your preference, a non-metallic or metallic gasket can be used, following application of suitable gasket sealer/cement. Any overlapping at the intake ports should be trimmed off. End seals can be made with a fairly thick cork; they'll compress and seal effectively when the manifold is bolted down and won't slide out.

For convenience, heavier engine parts such as flywheel and clutch, starter, etc. can be bolted to the engine before it's mounted in the body.

In the electrical department, a heavy 12-volt truck battery might be a good replacement for the stock 12-volt box. If you're primarily interested in racing applications, give some thought to relocating it in the truck to help traction. A standard, though longer, battery cable can be hooked up to the battery's positive pole and run to the starter solenoid terminal. To eliminate the stock key-type ignition switch, a 14-gauge wire can be run directly from the starter pole to a heavy duty toggle switch on the dash. Delco's resistor (#1957154), coil (#1115202), distributor (#194-2654) and rotor (#1932015) with brass contact points (not aluminum) plus condenser (#1932004) pretty well make up the component list in this department. Heat-resistant spark plug wires should be used — or Packard 440 wiring. Terminals should be attached with a crimping tool or securely soldered. With these modifications to the ignition chain, Autolite AT-2 spark plugs are effective spark producers.

The vacuum control should be eliminated from the stock distributor, and the point plate has to be anchored. The standard point assembly

should be replaced with the heavy duty assembly (#1966294), which incorporates extra-strong springs, thereby reducing point bounce. The stock setting provides full automatic advance of about 24 crankshaft degrees at 4000 rpm, so no modification to this curve is necessary.

With this *hot* setup, a great deal of importance should be placed on keeping the engine *cool*. During race applications, the fan would be omitted, but the stock radiator and water pump (with impellers intact) should be retained. A high-rpm pulley belt kit (deep-grooved pump and crank pulleys with a special racing belt) functions efficiently without an idler pulley. This combination will provide relatively trouble-free operation and suitable cooling.

With all this work — and attending diminishment of bank account — what can be expected in the way of action? After a suitable break-in, starting with the "grandma inch-along process" and progressing to harder runs, rings should be seated properly and other engine parts seated and/or mated accordingly. Checks should be made along the way for possible leaks of oil or water. Relatively hot plugs (such as Autolite AT-5's) should be used during this break-in to keep everything sharp and clean during the "take it easy" time. The colder plugs can be installed afterward. Yeah, but what about results? Well, engines prepared by the above techniques, along with suspension, transmission, tire selection and attending alterations all in the "legal" vein have turned sub-11-second e.t.'s and very close to 130-mph figures.

A final word? How about zymurgy? If it's good enough to wind up Webster's collection, it's good enough for us. . . .

By Don Green and Terry Cook

Performance-wise, Chevy's new "giant" small-block
disproves the old adage, "There's no substitute for cubic inches,"
but there are still ways to harness a . . .

400 inch bust

THE PEOPLE AT CHEVROLET HAVE GOT TO BE "NUMERO UNO" AT GETTING THE LONGEST LIFE OUT OF THEIR ENGINE DESIGNS. In the fifteen years they've been producing V8 engines, they've had only three basic designs, two of which are still very much alive. Only the 348-409 engine design has disappeared from the option lists. Of the two remaining engine designs, the undisputed longevity champ is their "small block." Since 1955, it has undergone a multitude of bore/stroke changes and design refinements, having been a 265, 283, 302, 307, 327 and 350-incher.

Now it's 1970, and that same small block Chevy engine is still with us. But the only thing that is small about the small-block is its exterior size. Inside, it's a giant! The engineers at Chevy have bored and stroked that high winding little engine all the way out to 400 cubic inches — a 4.125 inch bore and a 3.75 inch stroke, a considerable increase from the 3.750 x 3.00 inch 265 cube '55 block. Is nothing sacred?

If you've been looking through your Chevy dealer's sales materials, you've probably noticed that there are *two* 400 cubic inch engines in the lineup this year. One, of course, is the new small-block we've been speaking of, with its 2-bbl. carb and 265 horsepower. The other, a 4-bbl./355 horsepower version, is a *completely* different animal. It is basically a low-performance 396 with a slight over-bore, and offers less performance than the standard 396. Here, however, we are only involved with the small-block 400 design.

Known at Chevy plants and dealerships across the country as RPO LF-6, the small-block 400 is a stone! Don't get us wrong, though — Chevrolet intended it that way. They wanted a high-torque, low-rpm engine that would run on regular gas while pushing any of Chevy's heavier entries down the freeway. And they got it!

Performance-wise, Chevy's engineers will be the first to tell you that the LF-6 is not "where it's at," as far as its production components are concerned. For openers, forget the carburetor, intake manifold, cylinder heads and camshaft, as they are all low-performance items that have no racing applications. When we start looking into the short block, however, things begin getting a little more interesting, but only a little. The pistons are conventional cast, low-compression production items, and are extremely heavy when compared to the current crop of racing pistons. But they are ideal for the 400's designed purpose. At low rpm, they should last forever. Give the 400 a good high-rpm cam and some carburetion and the increased rpm would pull those same stock pistons apart.

The connecting rods are forged, but are made of the same 1046 steel mate-

(continued on following page)

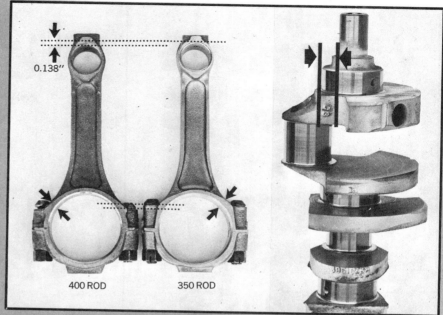

FIG. 1 — 400 rod is shorter in overall length; bolt boss is shorter and weaker.

FIG. 2 — Large 2.650-inch main bearings overlap with rod journals adding strength.

FIG. 3 — Small holes between cylinders carry water from block to heads, and must be plugged when using high-performance (non-400) small-block heads — tapered brass or lead plugs can be used; large bore causes "siamesing" of adjoining cylinders.

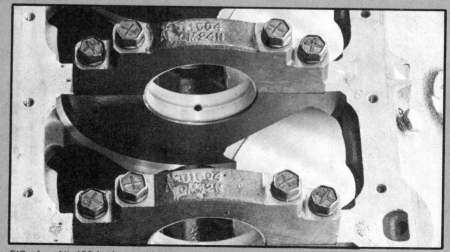

FIG. 4 — All 400-inch small-block Chevys are produced with the proven 4-bolt mains.

FIG. 5 — Center crank is stock 400 unit; at right is the original rough forging; at left is the counterweighted CSC destroker.

FIG. 6 — CSC modifies stock, rough rod forgings for added durability; includes polishing of sides to reduce cracking.

FIG. 8 — Stock cast piston is shown with CSC's forged racing piston having unique "head-land" rings and "Fire-Slot" dome design; stock pistons are extremely heavy.

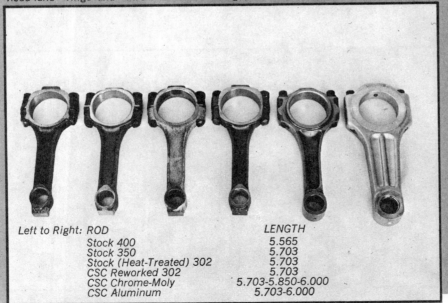

Left to Right:

ROD	LENGTH
Stock 400	5.565
Stock 350	5.703
Stock (Heat-Treated) 302	5.703
CSC Reworked 302	5.703
CSC Chrome-Moly	5.703-5.850-6.000
CSC Aluminum	5.703-6.000

rial used in all of Chevy's standard, low-performance production rods. And even though the 400's stroke has been increased a little over a quarter-of-an-inch from the longest production small block crank previously available from Chevy, the connecting rod length is actually shorter than any previous small block rod. The center to center length for the 400's rods is 5.565 inches, while all other small block Chevy rods are 5.703 inches long. (figure 1) If you recall our *Tech Series* article on connecting rods in last month's issue, it was pointed out that long rods, rather than shorter ones, is the plan. The shorter rod creates a severe rod angle, increasing the piston's side thrust and causing additional (undesirable) cylinder wall loadings. But it is also a characteristic of the shorter rod to produce increased low rpm torque. With that in mind, it is easier to understand Chevy's thinking behind the shortening of the small-block rods. While there may be some oddball custom engine situation which requires a shorter rod (we can't think of any, offhand), the short 400 rod is otherwise useless for performance applications. Another bad point is that the bolt bosses on the 400 rod have been shortened. When compared to the other late-model small block rods, this represents a loss of strength in the critical area near the bolt head (figure 1).

The 400-incher's crankshaft is also a departure from other late-model small-block Chevy cranks. While everything from the 250 hp/327 on up has been produced with a forged steel crank, Chevy has switched back to nodular cast iron for the 400's crank. Again though, the crank is perfectly suited to its designed function—low-rpm operation. At 3.75 inches, it is the longest stroke crankshaft ever produced by the factory for the small-block engine family, and provides a tempting piece of raw material for a moderate performance street machine. For use in an earlier (non-400) block, the new, larger-than-ever 2.650 inch diameter mains must be machined down to the usual small-block sizes of 2.450 or 2.300 inches. These larger mains have two effects on the crankshaft and its usage. Larger mains mean larger bearings and more bearing surface, and to a racer that means more bearing speed, more potential friction and more drag. For that reason, it is extremely common to find racers using the pre-'68 block and crankshaft assemblies with the smaller 2.300 inch diameter mains, which understandably have less bearing drag. But the large mains offer increased rigidity to the crank, as the diameter of the mains overlaps with the diameter of the crankpins at the ends of the throws (see figure 2). This provides a stiffer crank and reduces the torsional vibration during operation, resulting in less flexing and cracking. For an engine of this size (cubic inches) and considering the horsepower potential, the benefit of the added crank strength may offset any disadvantage of the increased bearing surfaces.

Like all the "big-block" 454's, the 400 inch small block is externally balanced. Rather than making the balance compensations on the crankshaft itself, Chevy has used the damper on the front of the crank and the flywheel on the rear to control the balance. While the husky 454 cranks are rigid enough to handle it, the more spindly 400 crank becomes subject to a great deal of flexing by having all the balance weights at the extreme ends, even with the overlapping main and rod journals.

While the 400 is made up of many new parts, none of the ones we've mentioned so far really lend themselves to high-performance work. But we've saved the best part for last — the cylinder block. The LF-6's 4.125 inch bore has never been possible before with any of Chevy's small blocks (without extensive sleeving). To make it possible for the 400, Chevy re-cored the casting, providing so much material around the cylinder bores that the metal actually flows together between each cylinder producing what are referred to as "siamesed" cylinders (see figure 3). There is no longer any provision for water to flow between the cylinders — that area has become a web of solid iron, but the web produced by the siamesed cylinders also adds a good deal of strength to the block, helping the cylinders resist flexing. Chevy has left enough material in the casting around the cylinder bores to easily allow a 0.030 inch overbore, while some have been successfully bored as much as 0.060 inches over stock, though 0.060 over is not recommended due to the lack of suitably large head gaskets. And all this with Chevy's already race-proven 4-bolt mains (figure 4).

So we now have a cylinder block that offers us something never before available from a factory-produced small-block Chevy — a huge 4.125 inch bore. And since the factory has designated it as a non-performance engine for the present, it remains for the speed equipment industry to carry the ball. And one of the men who has quickly begun a performance development program based around the LF-6 is Hank Betchloff of the Crankshaft Company in Los Angeles. Hank has already gone into production on a line of forged crankshafts to *destroke* the 400-incher, taking advantage of its big bore and giving it the kind of stroke that will let the small-block do what it has always done best — go for that high-rpm (by reducing piston travel). The CSC cranks are available. But for all-out high-performance use, CSC has the *short stroke*

forged cranks available either in their fully-counterweighted "Dyna-Rev" style or their non-counterweighted "Ultra-Rev" (figure 5).

FIG. 7 — Stock cast 400 piston (left), and CSC's forged flat top racing piston.

FIG. 9 — Head-land rings are of dykes design; placed at extreme top of piston sides; good low and high rpm sealing.

CSC can also provide the longer rods needed to make the engine perform well in the upper rpm ranges without changing displacement; anything from mildly reworked stock rods to their own superduty, forged, chrome-moly steel or forged aluminum rods. In the 2.100 inch crank pin size, they rework the 5.703 inch long 350 cube Chevy rods, selecting the hardest ones after Rockwell testing and magnafluxing; all rod bolt surfaces are milled parallel to the rod cap parting line; rod bolt holes are rebored parallel and enlarged to use 3/8 inch o.d. bolts rather than the stock 11/32 inch bolts; an even radius is cut around the rod bolt head and nut to relieve stress; and the forging lines are removed from the rod and the sides polished in the proper lengthwise manner (figure 6) followed by a complete able in three basic strokes: 3.000; 3.250; and 3.480 inches, comparable with the 283, 327 and 350 stock cranks, and all have the large 2.650 inch mains. All three use the 2.100 or 2-1/16 inch rod

journals. Working with an LF-6 block with a 0.004 inch clean-up bore, the possible displacements are 321.3, 348.1 and 372.7 cubic inches. What's so unusual about that, you ask? True, you've been able to get very nearly these same displacements from small-block Chevy's long before now, without the 400 cylinder block, but now you're getting these displacements with a full one-quarter inch *shorter* stroke than ever before.

Now do you see the light? That 350 cubic inch small-block you've been racing with its 4.00 inch bore and 3.48 inch stroke can now be replaced by a CSC equipped small-block with 348 cubic inches from a 4.129 inch bore and a much shorter 3.250 inch stroke. Or bore the block 0.030 inches over and get 352.5 cubes with that same short stroke. If you've been running a 327 with a 4.00 inch bore and 3.25 inch stroke, CSC can fix you up with a 321 inch engine with a quarter-inch shorter 3.000 inch stroke. Or bore the 400 block 0.030 over and the 3.000 inch crank will give you 325 cubic inches. And who can doubt that the CSC setup is going to be good for a gob more rpm than the stock 350 or 327.

For the guy who is looking for a particular cubic inch size engine to give his car the best break in a certain class, CSC reworks the basic short stroke cranks to offer stroke variations amounting to plus or minus about five cubic inches from the basic cranks. This gives you a ten or eleven cubic inch latitude in your engine's displacement, and is made possible by grinding the crank pins undersize to 2.000 inches and slightly off center. If you want a few *more* cubic inches, you grind the new rod journal to the *outside* of the original journal; if you want a few *less* cubes, grind the journal to the *inside* of the original. So, with a 4.129 inch bore, CSC can vary the stroke of the basic 3.250 inch crank to yield from 316 to 326.7 cubic inches. Likewise, the basic 3.480 inch crankshaft, when used with a 0.060 inch overbore of 4.187 inches, can be modified to give a total displacement varying between 377.8 and 388.2 cubic inches.

If all you want is just a good moderate performance crank based around the stock 400's 3.75 inch cast crank, CSC can give it their standard "Ultra-Rev" treatment. This includes cross-drilled mains, fully radiused mains and throws, and with optional Tuff-Triding, will provide a suitably strong crank for a moderate performance, high-torque

(continued on page **84**)

Chevy small V-8

307 to 400 Cubic Inches
265 to 370 Horsepower

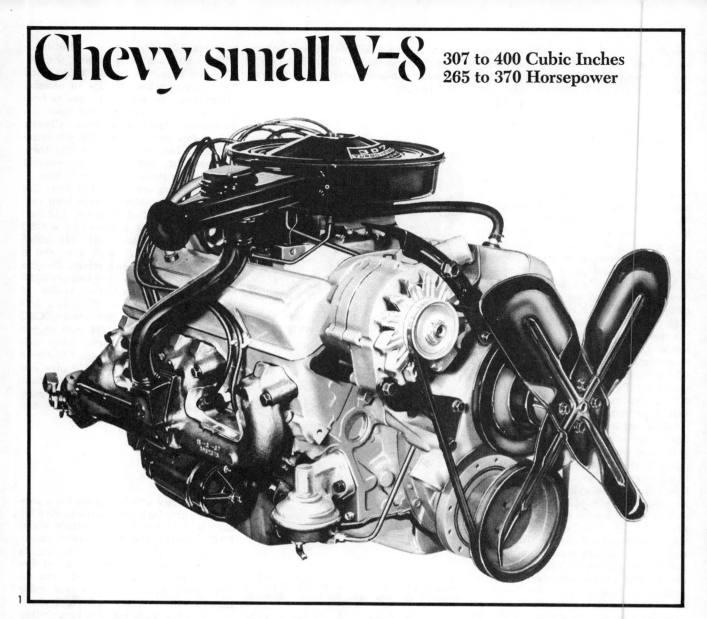

1

Chevy's small V-8 series started with the 265-cu.-in. engine in 1955, which was later bored to the popular 283. Neither of these engines have been available in recent years. Two displacement versions of the small V-8 series have been dropped for 1970—the Z-28 Trans-Am 290/302 and the two 327-cu.-in. engines which were the last of this displacement left last year. The 327 was basically a bored 307, with the same 3.25-in. stroke. The 5 different horsepower varieties of the 350-cu.-in. engine have the same stroke as the 327, at 4:000 ins., but a 3.48-in. bore. The one oddball of the 1970 series is the 265-hp regular gas 400-cu.-in., small-block V-8, which is both larger in bore and stroke than the 350 engines. The obvious connection between all of these small-block engines is the 4.40-in. bore spacing, center-to-center, against the 4.84 in. of the big block V-8's. For 1970 the "Z-28" engine is a 360-hp 350-cu.-in., which keeps it out of the SCCA's Trans-American Championship sedan races, with their displacement limit of 305 cu. ins. As the 302-cu.-in. race engine was basically a 283 crank in a 327 block, (which is the same as the 350 block), new 302's can still be assembled from these parts. The new 370-hp 350-cu.-in. Corvette engine is part Z-28 and part straight 350 series, or about half Z-28. For example, the valves are the same head size as the normal 350's, yet the cam profile, valve

timing, and valve gear are straight Z-28. If it's half Z-28, it might be called a Z-14, but it isn't; it's called an LT-1.

GENERAL / This series of engines are all 90° V-8's, with cast iron blocks and heads, and with 4.40-in. center-to-center bore spacing. Cylinders are numbered 1-3-5-7 on the left bank and 2-4-6-8 on the right, starting from the front. Firing order is 1-8-4-3-6-5-7-2. Three are regular gas engines, with horsepower in the 200-265 range, and a nice spread of torque variation. In the 350-cu.-in. size there are high-performance engines, all with 11.0:1 compression ratios, with claimed horsepowers of 350, 360 and 370. This last figure is most likely true for all 3. The engine code, such as F0013CNC, is stamped on a machined pad at the front of the right bank. The displacement and

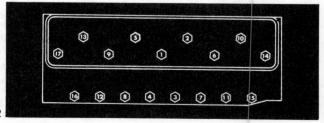

2

26

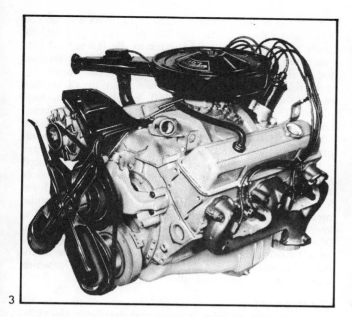

3

4

5

6

1. The 307-cubic-inch Turbo-Fire V-8 is presently the smallest V-8 available in the Chevrolet line, both in power output and displacement.

2. As with most engines, you start in the center and work toward both ends in progressive steps until all head bolts are at 65 ft.-lb. Follow this sequence closely to avoid danger of warpage.

3. The 307, while still in a very mild state of tune, has seen more than 15 years of development, beginning as a 265. It is an engine of many applications.

4. For 1970, the famed Z-28 option now displaces 350 cubic inches, instead of the 302 of 1969.

5. The 370-hp, 350-cubic-inch LT-1 is the most powerful of the small-block Chevrolets currently offered.

6. Quite popular as a sturdy, compact yet reliable engine is the 300-hp Turbo-Fire 350 engine, with 4-barrel carburetor and hydraulic valve lifters.

7. The 250/350 small-block Chevrolet is much the same as the stronger 300/350 except for its 2-barrel carburetor and slightly lower compression ratio

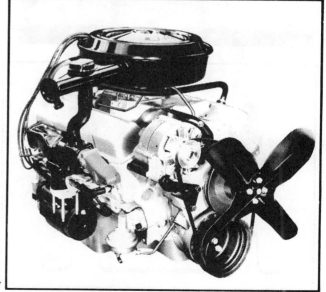

7

Chevy small V-8

horsepower are indicated by the 2 or 3 letters at the end of this code group.

200/307: CNC, CND, CNE, CNF, CNG, CNH, DA, DE, DC and DD.

250/350: CNI, CNM, CNN, CNO, CNU, CNV, CNY, CNZ, CNP, CNW, CNX, HC, HD and HF.

300/350: CNJ, CNK, CRE, CNQ, HA, HB, HE, HY, HZ, HP, CNR, CNS and CNT.

350/350: HW, HX.

265/400: CGR, CRH, CZX.

Previous years may have used the same engine code, so for positive identification of a 1970 engine, refer to the serial number stamped on the clutch housing left-side flange rear face, or next to the engine code. The second character is the model year, with "0" used for 1970, as in 10T100253.

PISTONS / The 200/307, the 250/350 and the 300/350 use cast aluminum alloy pistons with flat, notched heads. The higher-performance 350/350, 360/350 and 370/350 engines use impact-extruded aluminum pistons with domed heads and valve cutouts. The 265/400 engine is a regular grade gasoline engine, and is back to the flat-topped cast aluminum slugs. As is true of almost all Chevy engines today, all compression rings are cast iron. The upper ring is barrel-faced, with a molybdenum inlay in all engines except the 250/350 and 300/350, which are chromium-plated. The lower compression ring has an inside bevel and a tapered face with a wear-resistant coating on the 200/307, 250/350, 300/350 and 265/400 and chromium plating on the other 350 engines. The oil ring is always a multi-piece assembly, with 2 steel rails, chrome-plated on the outer surface, and a stainless steel expander-spacer in between. All piston pins are chromium steel, and are locked into the connecting rod small-end with a hydraulic press. The piston pins are offset in the pistons in the lower-performance engines, and on center in the 350-, 360- and 370-hp versions. The connecting rods are drop-forged steel with steel-backed, removable, premium aluminum big-end bearings in all but the 200/307, which uses sintered copper-lead alloy.

CRANKSHAFT / The lower-performance engines in the series use cast nodular iron crankshafts, with the 350-,

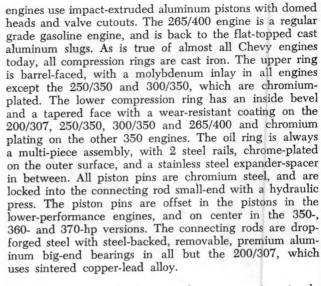

7

8

360- and 370-hp versions using forged steel. All run in 5 main bearings, identical in dimension except for the 360 and 370, which are different by a matter of ten-thousandths. All main bearings are removable, steel-backed, and can be either copper-lead alloy or premium aluminum lined, dependent on application.

CAMSHAFT / All camshafts are cast alloy iron, running in 5 removable, steel-backed babbitt bearings in the center of the vee, directly above the crankshaft. A 46-link timing chain connects the nylon-toothed aluminum camshaft gear with the steel sprocket on the front of the crankshaft. The valve timing of the cams is identical for the 200/307, 250/350 and 300/350; the 350/350 has a separate cam profile; the 360/350 and 370/350 are the same.

VALVES / Valves throughout the small V-8 engines are pretty much the same, the two exceptions being the 200/307 with its smaller diameter heads, and the 360/350

9

1. Crankshafts for the lower compression Chevrolet V-8's are made of cast nodular iron. For high-performance applications, forged crankshafts are available.

2. The LT-1 block for 1970 has 4-bolt main bearing caps. Note also the oil delivery holes directed to each one of the 5 bearing surfaces.

3. This is the high-rise manifold for the 1970 LT-1.

4. More LT-1 parts—the rocker covers are cast and finned.

5. Particularly valuable for high-rpm use is this goodie— a pushrod guide plate with screw-in rocker studs.

6. Pistons are available for the small-block Chevy engine in both high- and low-dome configurations.

7. Deck of the LT-1 small-block is similar to that on other Chevrolet small-blocks throughout the years.

8. In many cases, engine identification would be much easier if the numbers were located up front as on this Chevy.

9. The 265-hp, 400-cubic-inch engine is designed to give good, "torquey" service on regular gasoline.

10. Whoever thought that the small, 265-incher of 1955 would ever be punched out to 400 cubic inches?

10

Chevy small V-8

Z-28 with larger diameter heads. All engines use hydraulic valve lifters except the 360/350 (Z-28) and 370/350 (LT-1), which use solid lifters. Intake valves are alloy steel, exhaust valves are high alloy steel with aluminized faces. All use spring dampers inside the normal valve springs for both intake and exhaust.

LUBRICATION / Main bearings, connecting rod big-end bearings, camshaft bearings and hydraulic lifters are lubricated by oil under pressure in the oil galleries in the block. Piston pins get their oil by crankshaft splashing, the cylinder walls by cross-spray jets, and the timing chain and gears by oil centrifugally forced from the front camshaft bearing. The 4 qts. of oil in the crankcase are circulated by a gear-driven mechanical pump at 40 psi at 2000 rpm through a throwaway full-flow filter. Factory-recommended oils for operating temperatures above 20°F are SAE 20W, SAE 10W-30, SAE 10W-40 or SAE 20W-40.

1. The purpose of the small holes between the bores on this 400-incher is to let air and steam escape from the narrow recesses of the cooling jacket.

2. Stock Chevrolet crankshafts don't have center counter-weights. Illustrated here is a C&T crank. Note the off-center weights on both the front pulley and the flywheel.

3. This area of the 400-cubic-inch small-block is solid iron. It is called a siamese casting. Not too much room for gasket surface, is there?

4. It's a small-block but the 3 freeze plugs on each side show that it is a new casting—a 400-incher for '70.

FUEL SYSTEM / A mechanical fuel pump on the right front of the engine block works at 7.50-9.00 psi, except for the 200/307 which works at 5.50-7.00 psi. Filtering is done by a fine-mesh plastic strainer in the gas tank and a paper element filter in the carburetor inlet. All carburetors are Rochesters except for the 360/360 Z-28 and the 370/350 LT-1 Corvette, which use quad-throat Holleys. Idle speeds vary through the series, but are approximately 700 for manual transmission, excepting the Z-28 which should be set at 800. With an automatic transmission, most are around 600 for everything but the Z-28, which is set at 750.

3

4

CHEVROLET SMALL V-8	200/307 V-8	250/350 V-8	300/350 V-8	350/350 V-8	360/350 V-8	370/350 V-8	265/400 V-8
Displacement (cu. in.)	307	350	350	350	350	350	400
Horsepower @ rpm	200 @ 4600	250 @ 4800	300 @ 4800	350 @ 5600	360 @ 6000	370 @ 6000	265 @ 4400
Horsepower per cu. in.	.650	.715	.855	1.000	1.03	1.06	.660
Torque (lb.-ft.) @ rpm	300 @ 2400	345 @ 2800	380 @ 3200	380 @ 3600	380 @ 4000	380 @ 4000	400 @ 2400
Bore	3.875	4.000	4.000	4.000	4.000	4.000	4.125
Stroke	3.25	3.48	3.48	3.48	3.48	3.48	3.75
Compression Ratio	9.0:1	9.0:1	10.25:1	11.0:1	11.0:1	11.0:1	9.0:1
Carburetion	2-bbl.	2-bbl.	4-bbl.	4-bbl.	4-bbl.	4-bbl.	2-bbl.
1970 Engine Code	See General	See General	See General	See General	—	—	See General
Length/Width/Height (in.)	28/25/22	28/25/22	28/25/22	28/25/22	28/25/22	28/25/22	28/25/22

Text and photos by Bud Lang ■ Chevrolet introduced two new low-performance (hydraulic-cammed) engines earlier in this model year, both of 400-cubic-inch displacement. One is based on the small-block "mouse" motor, the other on the 396 "rat" motor; but unfortunately for performance enthusiasts, they were developed as high-torque, low-rpm workhorses. Fitted with a two-barrel carb, the "little" 400 cranks out 265 hp, while the "big" 400 does its best when delivering 350. What with their cast cranks and pistons, to name but two parts, they're strictly for the street.

The only component worth considering is the small engine's cylinder block. So we'll treat you to a few goodies that have been developed to make this unit rate use in a performance vehicle. The four-bolt main cap feature on this block is desirable, but its greatest claim to fame is the super-large, 4.125-inch bore size, ⅜-inch larger than the original 265-inch block.

Beginning with one of these blocks, it's possible to produce a high-performance Chevy engine varying between 316.0 inches and 388.2 inches, depending upon the bore-and-stroke combination you settle on. If you order a block through your local Chevrolet sports department, ask for the fitted block assembly (parts No. 3977676). It comes with fitted pistons, pins, rings and cam bearings. While you won't be needing the piston assemblies, you're stuck with them. Your only salvation would be to order 50 bare blocks at a time. Yep, you read that one right! Don't fret, though, because CrankShaft Company in Los Angeles orders in quantity, and therefore they have plenty of bare blocks to go around, along with their crank assemblies.

The biggest single advantage to be gained in choosing a 400-inch small-block as the basis of your engine is that it offers a better bore-to-stroke ratio than any of the other small-blocks. It also allows the engine to breathe better, due to its large bore size.

Running more bore than stroke results in less piston surface speed per minute while still providing an engine that is very responsive to the throttle, one that will rev instantly. You'll also find that there will be less piston rock and better ing sealing with this combination. This is a prime reason Chevrolet developed a new 430-inch engine when they already had a good 427. The 427, with its 4.25-inch bore and 3.76-inch stroke, offers a ratio of only 1.13:1, which isn't too good. Chevy's new 430-inch Can-Am engine, on the other hand, features a 4.440-inch bore and 3.470-inch stroke, for a ratio of 1.28:1. By cleaning up the 400's cylinder bores .004-inch (for a new bore of 4.129) and slipping in a 3.250-inch stroke crank (thereby destroking the 400 by ½-inch), we arrive at a total displacement of 348.1 inches, with a bore/stroke ratio of 1.27:1. This figure just about matches the potent 430. If you are wondering why you should go to a custom-built 348, when Chevy also has a 350, then let's compare this engine, too. The 350 has a 4.00-inch bore and 3.480-inch stroke, for a ratio of only 1.15:1. We've already given reasons why you should want a "favorable" bore/stroke ratio, but let's see if the racers agree.

Bill "Grumpy" Jenkins and his super-hot Camaros need no introduction. He took three major championships earlier this year on three successive weekends, against the best in the country, and he's running one of these 430s with CrankShaft Company components in his Pro Stocker. Another racer, Carroll Caudle, runs a '55 Chevy in D/MP and holds the class mph record at 124.96. He's presently using a 400-inch block with the CSC 348-inch assembly just mentioned. Running in excess of 8000 rpm, he is consistently running over his mph mark now and in the 11.0s against an 11.36 record.

According to Hank Bechtloff of CrankShaft, the ratio between actual connecting rod length and the overall stroke is equally important, with ratios between 1.75:1 and 2.0:1 recommended and 1.85:1 preferred. We find this ratio by dividing the rod length (center-to-center length between bores) by the stroke. Let's take the CSC 348-inch "400" block again.

The ratio, if 5.700-inch-long rods are used in conjunction with a 3.250-inch stroke, is 1.75:1. Now if we were to utilize a 5.850-inch-long rod, the ratio would increase to 1.80:1 — a bit more favorable. Here are the reasons why: Up to a point, long connecting rods are preferable, because they reduce chances of piston wobble in the bores and offer less side thrust to the pistons (which would increase cylinder wall flexing), but they also increase leverage on the throws, thereby providing an improved torque range. With long rods you can also experiment slightly with cam timing. Of course if the connecting rods are too long, these latter benefits would be negated. Run rods that are too short and you end up overloading the cylinder walls, because of severe rod angle.

CrankShaft Company offers a number of cranks for the 400 block. Their Series "E" cranks come with either 2.00-,

It may not look like much in its stock surroundings, but Chevy's 400-inch mini-rat is loaded with performance potential

Chevy's MINI-RAT

2¹⁄₁₆- or 2.100-inch-diameter throws in strokes of 3.00, 3.250 or 3.480 inches. They also offer Series "F", "G" and "H" cranks, all with 2.00-inch-diameter throws, in strokes of between 2.950 or 3.530 inches. All these forged steel cranks are CSC "Dyna-Revs." Designed for the serious racers, they are fully counterweighted; feature cross-drilled mains and chamfered oil holes; are heat-treated, indexed, magnetic-inspected and Tuff-Trided; and feature their large "UDR" radius.

Stock 400 connecting rods are steel forgings, but they are not heat-treated to a high Rockwell "C" reading and have many other shortcomings relative to high-performance use. Again, whereas the 400 features a stock stroke slightly more than a quarter-inch longer than any previous small-block Chevy, the connecting rod length is actually shorter. The

(Continued on following page)

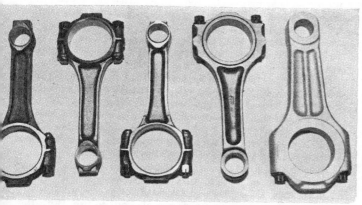

ABOVE — To the left is a stock cast 400 crankshaft. While good for supermarket trips, it can't compete with the CSC forged steel shaft to its right. This unit is fully counterweighted and finished for racing. It's available in different strokes. A complete assortment of connecting rods are available, although all but stocker are recommended. From the left, we find them to be stock 400-incher, again, strictly for stock usage; a CSC refinished 302 rod for 2.00-inch crankpins; another refinished high-performance 302 rod (this one for 2.100-inch pins); one of CSC's forged chrome moly steel rods (the ultimate) and last, their forged aluminum rod. Both the forged steel and aluminum units are available in different center-to-center lengths. If you adapt other cylinder heads to your 400 block, be sure to use the 400 head gaskets as template and drill two holes (arrows) between each combustion chamber set to allow steam passage. This head is from a 327 Chevy and has been reworked by Air Flow Research. Again we find a comparison between stock and high-performance parts in the pistons fitted in the 400 cylinder block at left. The stock cast unit, with its dished top and double valve reliefs, is just the ticket for low-compression running. The forged aluminum slug is one by CrankShaft Company, complete with flame slot, full dome and valve reliefs of a size commensurate with the valve sizes. When assembling an engine, it's mighty important to check clearances. Here, bearings get checked out.

MINI-RAT

other small-block rods are 5.700 inches in length, yet the 400 rod is only 5.565 inches, or .135-inch shorter. Therefore we find that the rod-length-to-stroke ratio on the stock 400 combination is only 1:48:1, considerably off from our desired 1:85:1 figure.

To offset these problems, CSC offers the engine builder a choice of three distinct connecting rods, most available in different rod lengths and/or crank pin bore diameters. If you're going to be running a crank with 2.100-inch crank pins, then you have a choice of two factory rods, both 5.700 inches long. These are late 350 and 302 rods. One set of 302s is also available for use with 2.00-inch crank pins. Both can be had fully refinished and ready for high-performance work. These race-ready rods have been carefully selected after Rockwell testing for hardness and magnafluxing. They have forging marks removed by polishing, feature parallel-milled rod bolt and nut surfaces and radiused bolt and nut seats; and have been shot-peened. All these operations are performed to increase rod strength and longevity.

If you don't have too much faith in stock rods, then CSC offers super-duty forged E 4340 chrome moly rods. Considerably higher in cost, these units also give you considerably more strength, safety and peace of mind. These forged

chrome moly rods are available in three standard lengths, fitting either 2.00-, 2¹⁄₁₆- or 2.100-inch crank pins. Their lengths are: 5.700, 5.850 and 6.00 inches. If you would rather save a little weight and still retain strength, then try their forged aluminum rods. Their 6.00-inch rod (.300-inch longer than stock) is available for the same three crank pin sizes, while the standard-length, 5.700-inch, aluminum rod is available in either 2.00- or 2.100-inch sizes.

Just because we keep referring to this non-factory-standard crank pin size of 2¹⁄₁₆ inches (or 2.062 inches), don't let it throw you. It's something Hank Bechtloff cooked up with Mike Durella of Federal-Mogul. Wanting to improve the crank pin radius of the 2.100-inch crank, Hank had his new crew grind one of these cranks .038-inch undersize while correcting the stroke length and indexing the shaft. With a beautiful "blueprinted" crank on hand, he then had to come up with a bearing insert. That's when Mike developed a new high-performance engine bearing especially for this custom CSC crank pin size. Known as the 1840 AP racing insert, it's available through CSC for use with engines running special rods and '68 or later cranks modified to 2¹⁄₁₆-inch-diameter crank pins.

This bearing features a high-alloy steel back with a special lead-over-aluminum facing, offering superior bearing conformance and embedment characteristics. Thus it can be said that, in addition to being highly durable, it offers babbitt bearing characteristics by its ability to remove minute foreign elements from the oil before they have a chance to wipe out the bearing and possibly scour the crank journal.

In case any Ford lovers are reading this far into "Chevy territory," we might add that these same bearings can be used in 289s, Boss 302s and Cleveland 351s, providing CSC forged steel or aluminum rods are also put to use. With the 351 engine, you can also obtain a neat ¼-inch stroke increase by having the crank pins offset-ground in the process.

CSC also has a line of forged aluminum pistons in bore sizes ranging from stock to .030-inch over (.060 over on special order) in stock. Compression heights ranging from 1.800 to 1.250 inches, as measured from the pin center to piston deck, are also available. These units are available with any one of a number of ring combinations, including a new ring, called a "head-land" ring, that CSC has just come out with. Of Dykes design, this unit rides in a groove cut into the piston at its uppermost edge, just below the piston's deck surface. This high placement fully exposes the ring to the pressure in the cylinder, increasing its effectiveness. While this principle was the basis for designing this ring, one can't help wondering how long this ring design will function properly, since it is completely enveloped in flame every time the cylinder fires. Of low-tension design, the Dykes ring comes with a coil expander that allows wall tension to be set statically between 2 and 5 pounds.

The 400 cylinder block has two small holes between each set of cylinder bores on the block decks, for a total of six per side. These carry steam from the block up into the heads. If you're going to run heads other than the 400's, you should drill matching holes in the head surfaces, using the 400 gasket as a template. All other small-block components — manifolds, oil pump, pan, etc. — will bolt right on the 400. If you're using a CSC crank assembly in the 400 block, you can also make use of the 327 or 350 dampener and flywheel. But if you're contemplating using a complete stock 400 block assembly, bolting on your own small-block parts, you must run the 400 dampener and flywheel.

When one considers the immense amount of high-performance equipment available for the small-block Chevys, it doesn't take long to realize the advantages to be gained in using one of these 400s (with the "right" parts, of course). The few that are running with much of the equipment mentioned herein are doing right smartly, so there's no need to rave on. These engines may be pint-sized rats, but they're doing their share of roaring. ■■

The two pistons above, and the one at right below, are CSC "J" series slugs for 400 block. The offset dome (compare with small-block slug at left) stuffs the chamber better, and with skirt reliefs and buttons, it's hi-perf goody.

The Right Slant

Hopefully, for you do-it-yourselfers, the angle of the plug can be seen in these photos. As more complete combustion is sought for emission control, plug location and angle will soar in importance. Since all of this spells more heat in the chamber, crankshaft horsepower is bound to move on up.

Text and photos by John Thawley ■ Got a small-block Chevy? Want some more horsepower in the form of stock Chevy parts? No problem if you see your parts man at the Chevy dealer for the new trick "Trans-Am" head. The head is generally termed "Trans-Am" since it first saw the public light on the Jim Hall Trans-Am Camaros at St. Joviete. The new cylinder head is also referred to as the "slant-plug" head since, in fact, plug angle is the only modification made to the existing LT-1 head.

The angled-plug head is typical of the Chevrolet approach to problems and is well-suited to the small-block head. Keep in mind that, generally speaking, only gradual improvements and modifications have been made to achieve and maintain this cylinder head's outstanding performance since 1955 — and 16 years is a very long time in this business!

Sometime in early 1970, Chevrolet concluded it was desirable to improve the combustion efficiency of the small-block head again. They wanted to make the improvement without casting change or addition of metal or other hardware — not an easy task.

After no small amount of work, Chevy Engineering brought forth the new design which locates a 14mm taper-seat plug nearer the charge center and closer to the squish area.

The thinking was that maximum turbulence would be directed toward the plug, thus improving the speed of combustion and the resulting pressure rise which spells horsepower. By achieving optimum flame travel, maximum energy could be extracted from the incoming charges and transferred to the piston with a minimum of piston travel, since the amount of piston motion per degree of crank travel decreases at TDC.

All of this works just like the design extrapolations said it would, and the new head is now sold by Chevy dealers under parts No. 3965742. The new plug angle will not prevent the head from being used with anything you've got in the way of stock exhaust system or headers. In fact, the plug angle moves the plug boots and wires away from the exhaust and makes plug changing a little easier.

The icing on the cake is, naturally, the horsepower gained by angling the plugs. Initial dyno testing shows an increase of ten horsepower through the entire speed range versus the conventional plug location. Notice that we said initial dyno testing and entire speed range. At this writing, heads are on more than Trans-Am cars, and indications are that the heads are worth more than ten horses with some combinations of intake systems and camshafts.

Existing spark plug holes in the LT-1 heads can be plugged and a new plug-locating hole machined to turn old heads into the new slant-plug design. This is hardly a greasy garage floor operation, since it requires a cast iron plug, high-temperature epoxy and a mill with which to handle the machine work. If you come by a set of the new heads, install a set of spark plugs before the heads are installed, in order to locate any exposed tap threads in the chamber which might cause preignition. A further precaution in this regard can be taken by removing the first thread from plugs used in the new head.

What it all boils down to, Chevy fans, is more strain for the dyno or the rear end — just depends on where you like to put the power. ■ ■

Biceps for the Small-Block

*With all the special "heavy duty" parts that Chevy offers—
plus the equipment available from specialty manufacturers—you
can add muscle to your small V-8 for any performance need.*

By Roger Huntington

The hot rod industry provides more special speed equipment for the small-block Chevrolet than any other basic engine design. And the Chevrolet factory is not far behind. A tremendous amount of laboratory performance development has been done on this engine in the last 15 yrs., with the result that we have a long list of well engineered pieces of special equipment available to the Chevy builder today. Much of this equipment has never been used on production engines and is only available on special order over the counter through your neighborhood Chevrolet dealer.

We want to concentrate on this "factory" hop-up equipment right now. It may not seem right to try to divorce the factory equipment from "specialty" pieces originated by the hot rod industry. But there is such a choice in the factory equipment that you can easily mess up a good car with the wrong combination of parts, without ever going to a speed shop. We want to prevent that here and now.

The popular "performance" block right now is the 350-cu.-in. job as used in the Z-28 Camaro and LT-1 Corvette (Part No. 3966921 for short-block assembly). This has the 4-bolt main bearing caps and forged, Tuff-trided crankshaft that is desirable for all-out competition work. However, this kind of beef is not needed on the street. In fact, the hottest plan for street jobs right now is the new 400-cu.-in. utility engine. The engineers had to go to "siamesed" cylinder walls to squeeze the 4⅛-in. bore diameter into the short 4.40-in. bore center-to-center distance. A lot of guys predicted this would affect the cooling of the engine, or cause bore distortion that would bring rapid ring wear. But it hasn't happened. The guys are finding that this new 400 short block is great for a high-torque street engine of minimum size and weight. The 400 block does have 4-bolt main caps. However, it does not come with a forged crank. And you can't substitute the shorter-stroke 350 forged crank, because the main bearings are bigger in the 400 block. So the boys are going to the hot rod industry for special forged billet shafts when using the 400 block on the racetrack.

But you can feel confident about using it as is on the street, even with big heads, carburetion and a strong cam. It's beefier than we thought.

So right now you can hardly go wrong with either the 350 or 400 blocks, with or without the 4-bolt main caps and forged crank. (Actually most 350 blocks you would run across would have the 4-bolt caps, as they have been used on most 4-bbl. 350 engines for 3 yrs.)

LUBRICATION

Chevrolet uses a special 5-qt. baffled oil pan, windage baffle and high-capacity oil pump on Z-28 and LT-1 engines. These parts can all be bought and installed on any standard block. They are highly desirable on competition engines, and probably not necessary on the street. Suit yourself.

PISTONS AND RODS

In selecting connecting rods you have to remember that the crankpin journal diameter was increased from 2.00 to 2.10 ins. in 1968, with main journals up from 2.30 to 2.45 ins. So '67 and earlier cranks and rods will not interchange with the latest parts.

But Chevy supplies good pieces for both sizes. Their most exotic rod for the small block (Part No. 3946841) is for the large journal size, and features full-floating piston pin, ⅜-in. bolts and shot-peened surfaces. This was used in '69 Z-28's. Similar rods are also available for pressed pins, as used on later engines. These are all very strong rods, suitable for all-out competition work, and probably more than you need on the street.

Incidentally, if you have an earlier 302, 327 or 350 engine with the small rod journals, the good rod (used in '67 Z-28's) has Part No. 3927145. This has the pressed pin and the forging was shot-peened during manufacture of the rod. However, additional shot-peening, polishing, etc. will help if you feel you need it.

1. Late Corvette LT-1 350 engine, rated 370 hp, is the most powerful factory small-block engine, although the late "178" cam has knocked 10 hp off top end. Same engine as Z-28.

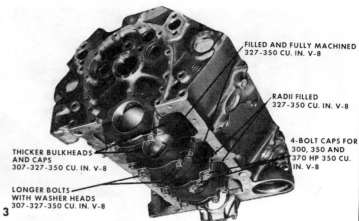

FILLED AND FULLY MACHINED
327-350 CU. IN. V-8

RADII FILLED
327-350 CU. IN. V-8

4-BOLT CAPS FOR
300, 350 AND
370 HP 350 CU.
IN. V-8

THICKER BULKHEADS
AND CAPS
307-327-350 CU. IN. V-8

LONGER BOLTS
WITH WASHER HEADS
307-327-350 CU. IN. V-8

2

3

4

2. Later high-performance blocks feature 4-bolt main bearing caps, heavy-duty bearings throughout and the Tufftrided crankshaft.

3. Improvements made on '68 and later blocks include larger bearings as well as improvements shown here.

4. The new 400-cu.-in. block has the "siamesed" cylinder walls, with no water jacket between, to allow the wide 4⅛-in. bore diameter in a 4.4-in bore spacing. There are no cooling or distortion problems.

5. Standard small-block Chevys use cast nodular iron crankshafts, with the high-performance models using forged, Tufftrided units.

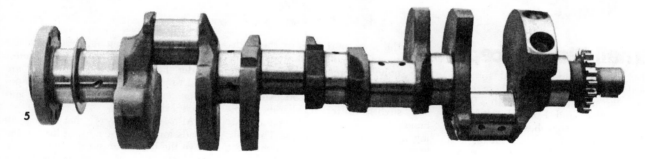

5

High-performance Corvette and Z-28 engines since the days of the 327 block have used good TRW forged pistons. These all had domed heads with notches for valve clearance, to get around 11:1 compression ratio with the 65cc's combustion chamber volume used in those days. The '71-'72 engines get 9.0:1 compression with flat-top pistons and about 75cc's of chamber volume, in the 350 displacement size. The larger chamber volume accounts for the bulk of this drop in compression, with the piston tops having a smaller effect. Thus, you could use earlier 65cc heads with late flat-top pistons and end up with maybe 10.5 compression in 350 size—where

the late 75cc heads and domed pistons would run closer to 9.5. Use the 65cc heads on a 327 or 350 block if possible, unless you have special pistons to compensate. On the other hand, the late 75cc heads on the 400 block, with flat pistons, would give well over 10:1. (The 400 normally uses dished pistons.) There are many possible combinations to choose from.

We won't take space to give a lot of part numbers for the various 302, 327 and 350 forged pistons and their oversizes. Suffice it to say that Chevrolet offers a full choice for the three different stroke lengths, with domes to match, and fitted for both floating and pressed pins. The floating pins

are definitely desirable for competition, though it's not critical on the street. However, it should be mentioned that the domes on Chevy factory pistons are not hefty enough to restore high compression if, say, you have "ported" out your combustion chambers maybe 7 or 8cc's to improve airflow around the valves. Then you have to go to the hot rod industry for high dome pistons. Factory pistons are designed strictly for factory combustion chambers.

CYLINDER HEADS

As mentioned earlier, there's a difference in chamber volume between the early high-performance heads and

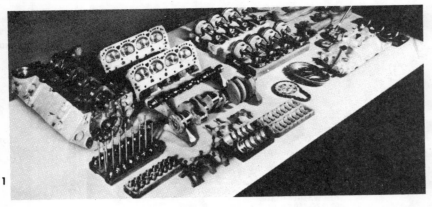

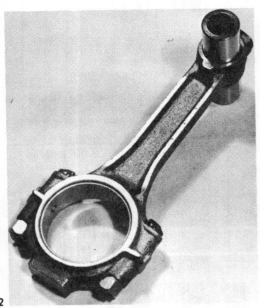

1. Dozens of special parts are needed to make a Z-28. These can be had over the counter to update any small-block if your money lasts.

2. Shot-peening is used on certain model connecting rods. Latest high-performance units have ⅜-in. bolts and are fitted for floating pins.

3. Rods found in the new 400 are slightly shorter to compensate for longer stroke without raising block deck height. Or standard 5.7-in. rod can be used with special piston. Stock 400 piston is dished out for smog-regulation low compression.

Small-Block Biceps

the '71-'72 heads designed for low-lead fuels. Otherwise all these heads have the same port sizes, with 2.02-in. intake valves and 1.60 exhausts. This basic head design has been around since 1964, so there are a lot of used heads on the market. Get the earlier type with 65cc chambers, if possible. The latest part number on this would be 3987376, which would be the one used on the Z-28 in 1970. If you're buying heads, this would be the one to get, as it also has screw-in rocker studs and pushrod guide plates attached under the studs. These plates prevent the pushrods from rubbing and wearing in the head bores, and can help prevent bent pushrods. And the screw-in studs don't pull out under high spring pressures. Good new features. (Incidentally, you can buy these new studs and guide plates separately, and install them in older heads with some minor machining. No problem at all.)

Many Chevy fans don't realize that the standard 327/350 heads have ex-

actly the same port sizes as the high-performance heads just mentioned. The only differences are that the standard heads have smaller valves —1.94-in. intakes and 1.50 exhausts— and slightly different chamber volumes. They also have the same casting mark, with two humps. The only way you can readily tell them apart is by measuring the valve diameters. The point is that these standard heads probably breathe a lot better than you think. If you can't readily find a set of the big-valve Corvette/Z-28 heads, or if the price is too stiff, you could do a lot worse than settling for the standard heads. They were used on practically all 4-bbl. 327 and 350 engines, and some 2-bbls. Look for the casting mark with two humps. There are millions of them around.

It should also be mentioned here that Chevrolet has recently released a new performance head for the 350 engine, with the spark plug inserted at a different angle to give better flame travel and quicker combustion in the small 65cc chamber. These heads have never been used on an

assembly line engine; but they are presently available over the counter under Part No. 3965742. They are said to give 15-20 hp more on competition engines with long cams and open exhaust.

Also don't forget that the new heads for the 400-cu.-in. utility engine have the big ports and the big 1.60-in. exhaust valves, in conjunction with the medium 1.94-in. intakes. This might be a good power/torque compromise for the 350 block except these heads have 75cc chambers, so compression would be a problem.

INTAKE MANIFOLDS

The very best all-around factory manifold for the small-block Chevy would be the late hi-riser aluminum 4-bbl. type used on Z-28/LT-1 engines (Part No. 3972114). This normally carries a 780 cfm Holley, and has large, smooth passages that are raised substantially, to ease the curve going into the head ports. And it has provisions for exhaust heat for cool weather (or you can block the heat risers in summer). This is a very good manifold for the street.

Don't confuse this late Z-28 manifold with the big-port aluminum 4-bbl. job that was used on some 327 Corvette engines in the mid-'60's. That had lower risers and more flow restriction at high revs. They say the new one gives 10-15 hp more above 5000 rpm, with similar carb capacity. The early aluminum 327 manifold is a lot better than the standard cast iron 4-bbl. design; but if you can afford the Z-28/LT-1 design, do it.

Chevrolet also offers a dual 4-bbl. "cross-ram" aluminum manifold for Trans-Am racing, similar to Edelbrock STR manifolds of this design. It has Part No. 3941124, and is designed to mount two 600 cfm Holleys, in a low profile that will fit under the standard Camaro hood. No exhaust heat, of course. It's strictly a competition manifold, not intended for the street. In fact, it isn't really a good bet for competition, unless the rules require a stock hood and no air scoop. If you can go higher, you're better off with one of the "hi-ram" Edelbrock or Weiand designs with inline 4-bbls. as used in Pro Stock and Modified Production drag racing.

Incidentally, the best 4-bbl. carburetor to use on the Z-28 manifold on the street is the 780 cfm Holley 3310 model that comes stock from the factory on Z-28 and LT-1 engines, with the vacuum-operated secondary throttles. It carries Part No. 3972121 when bought through a Chevy dealer. You can go to the 850 cfm Holley with 1¾-in. throttle bores on an all-out street engine in the 350 to 400-cu.-in. range, but preferably on a special manifold like the Edelbrock "Tarantula."

CAMS AND VALVE GEAR

Chevrolet offers four excellent factory camshafts for the small-block engine that should meet most of your high-performance needs:

Part No. 3863151—This is the hydraulic cam used in the popular 350-hp 327 Corvette engines in the mid-'60's, with 342° duration and .447-in. lift. It's the strongest hydraulic cam Chevy offers for the small-block. And yet it is mild enough for smooth low-speed response in everyday street driving, with a strong pull from 4000 to 5500 rpm. The upper rev limit is about 5800 with standard valve springs. You can buy it for $30 and slip it into any small-block engine, and use it with standard springs and lifters. One of your better horsepower-per-dollar buys in this field.

Part No. 3849346—This is the solid-lifter "30-30" Duntov cam used in 327 fuel injection engines and early Z-28's. It has 346° duration and .455-in. lift (allowing for the loss of lift due to normal valve lash). These specs don't look much more radical than the former hydraulic 350-hp cam. But the opening and closing rates are much quicker, so you have a lot more area under the lift curve, and this is what turns on the breathing at the top end. It also makes the cam more lumpy and less responsive at the bottom end. This is a marginal street cam in the 302 block. It works better in the 350 block, and is really sweet on the street in the 400 block. You can

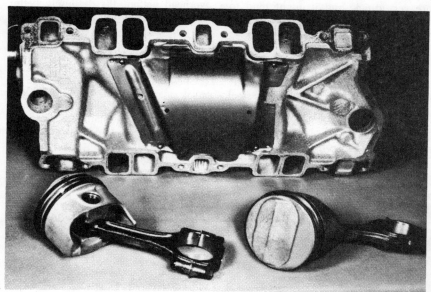

4. The new Z-28 high-riser alloy manifold is shown here with forged pistons and heavy-duty rods.

5. Intake port area on latest high-performance heads is 2.2 sq. ins., and pushrod guide plates and big 2.02-in. valves are featured.

6. Better flame propagation in the new canted spark plug heads is said to be worth 10-15 hp over old heads.

Small-Block Biceps

use this cam with the standard valve springs and mechanical lifters. The upper rev limit is about 6500 rpm with the standard stuff.

Part No. 3972178—Chevrolet engineers modified the above 30-30 cam for the new 350-cu.-in. Z-28 engine that came out in 1970. They left the exhaust lobes alone, but they shortened the intake timing to 317° duration and .435-in. lift. This gave a much smoother idle and more responsive low-speed performance on the street, with a loss of less than 10 hp above 5000 rpm. This is a beautiful street cam for the 302 and 350 blocks. But we prefer the above 30-30 cam for the 400. Incidentally, the upper rev limit is about the same for this cam (6500 rpm), and it is used with the standard valve springs and solid lifters.

Part No. 3927140—This cam is designed for the racetrack, not for the street. It's rated at 333°/346° duration and .475/.495-in. lift (intake/exhaust),

and should be used with special valve springs (Part No. 3972142). These are considerably stiffer than the standard springs, with 120 lbs. of pressure on the seat, compared with about 90 lbs. for standard springs. This extra tension allows 7500-8000 rpm without any distress in the valve gear. These springs can also be used with the other two solid-lifter cams listed above, to extend the useable rev range 1000 rpm. But we don't advise trying to use this "140" cam on the street, even in the 400-cu.-in. block. The rates are very quick, and it might tend to wear fast as well as give poor low-speed response. Keep it on the race-track where it belongs.

The factory Z-28 and LT-1 engines using these strong mechanical cams are fitted with special pushrods (Part No. 3796243), with hardened steel tips and special rockers (Part No. 3843359) with hardened and ground pallet tip. You can identify these by the letter "O" forged in the pallet tip. These parts are not absolutely essential when switching to a solid-lifter

cam, but you may want to make the addition for maximum reliability and durability under high-rev conditions.

It should also be mentioned here that, if ordering a set of mechanical lifters for replacement, be sure to get Part No. 5231585. These were used in 327 Corvette engines and the late 350 Z-28's; the oil feed to the overhead valve gear is controlled by a metering orifice in the lifter. The lifter used in the 302-cu.-in. Z-28's had a tiny inertia flap valve for oil feed, and this put quite a bit more oil up in the overhead action. It's definitely better to have less oil up here in a high-revving engine.

EXHAUST MANIFOLDS

Chevrolet never made a decent exhaust manifold for the small-block engine. Forget all about the various cast iron factory manifolds, and go directly to the hot rod industry for a good set of steel tubing headers. This is absolutely the first move you should make in hopping up any small-block

1. The original 302-cu.-in. engine in the Z-28's, introduced in 1967, was conservatively rated at 290 hp, but actually delivered that much at the flywheel on the road!

2. Holley 780-cfm 4-bbl. for Z-28 with vacuum secondaries has the optimum street response.

3. The factory cross-ram dual-quad carburetion system used on Trans-Am racers is a bolt-on kit. It's very strong between 5000 and 7000 rpm.

4. The ram-air system for cross-ram setup picked up cold air from the cowl's air plenum. This could probably be adapted to other Chevys.

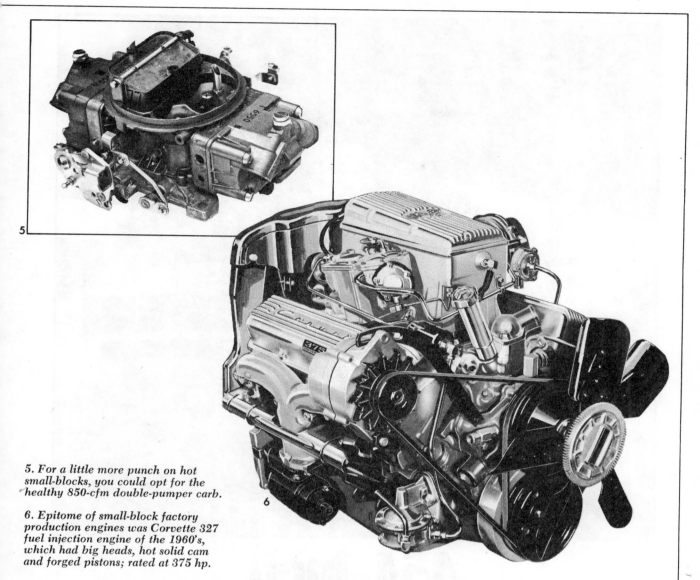

5. *For a little more punch on hot small-blocks, you could opt for the healthy 850-cfm double-pumper carb.*

6. *Epitome of small-block factory production engines was Corvette 327 fuel injection engine of the 1960's, which had big heads, hot solid cam and forged pistons; rated at 375 hp.*

Chevy, for either street or racetrack. There are literally hundreds of models to choose from, in dozens of companies, and prices are as low as $60 a set. You can hardly go wrong.

IGNITION

The ignition problem for hot street engines has been simplified in the last couple of years by the appearance of these bolt-on ignition kits to hop up a standard system. Usually they come with a hot coil, rotor and cap, hi-rev replacement points, and a condenser (sometimes spark plug wires are included). For $20 to $45 you can convert your factory ignition to "high-performance" in 30 mins. with one of these kits. Then just modify the centrifugal spark advance curve, with a kit or in your own shop, and you're ready to go. The usual recommendation for the small-block Chevy is to rework the curve 20°-24° advance in

the distributor, with maximum advance reached by 2500 rpm engine speed—then set initial advance at 14°-18°. Total should be 36° to 42°. You can play with the settings to see what the engine likes best.

If you want to go a step further with ignition refinement, Chevrolet supplies a complete Delco breakerless transistorized system that is great for either street or racetrack. The special distributor (Part No. 1111267) triggers the spark via a magnetic rotor and pickup, so there are no conventional breaker points to pit and burn and "float" at high revs. The accompanying kit (Part No. 3921048) includes a special high-output coil, a transistorized amplifier to boost the magnetic pulse to work the coil, and the necessary wiring harness and fittings. The total price is $194. But you get a really sophisticated ignition system that does away with the points and boosts high-rpm spark voltage at

the same time. It's as good as a magneto.

We wouldn't say that the stock factory ignition system for the small-block Chevy is any weaker or less adequate than most factory systems. It's a good one, in fact, and will do its job efficiently up to 6000 rpm—if you are careful to replace plugs and points regularly. The new aftermarket kits (Accel, Holley, Borg-Warner, Echlin, Sorenson, etc.) extend the effective range to 7000 rpm or more, and add some quality and durability not found in *any* factory system. Then you could consider the exotic transistorized system (with capacitor-discharge coil booster if you want) to be mostly for really all-out street and competition engines. You have a huge choice of equipment here.

In fact, it looks like Chevrolet has enough factory equipment in *every* area of the small-block engine to meet all your needs. ✠

454-inch
Small-Block CHEVY

The small-block takes on new status by growing as large as 482 cubic inches

TEXT AND PHOTOS BY DON GREEN ■ You'll find very few people who will argue with the statement that the small-block Chevy is the world's most popular performance engine. After being around in the same basic form for more than 17 years, most of the bugs have been worked out. Not that there were all that many bugs to begin with. Light, compact and capable of producing bunches of horsepower in relation to

its displacement and weight, the small-block Chevy has, at one time or another, found itself in virtually every type of racing vehicle from Indianapolis to Irwindale, Budd's Creek to Bonneville.

If anyone has ever had a complaint about the engine, it was generally that it was "too small." It simply couldn't be built into the large displacements that some people felt were necessary for particular forms of racing. The introduction of the 400-cubic-inch version of the small-block in 1970 helped quiet some of the critics, but development of the 400 has been slow due to the lack of factory - produced, performance - oriented engine parts (such as forged-

steel cranks and high-compression pistons). But even at 400 cubic inches, there are people who insist that the engine still isn't big enough or capable of being strong enough.

There's one guy around, however, to whom that thought hasn't even occurred. The only thing he knows is that small-block Chevys are the way to go, and if you work at it long enough, you're going to find a way to make them as big as you want. He's currently building and running small-blocks that range in displacement from 427 to 482 cubic inches, the most popular being a 454-cubic-inch version.

The man's name is Jack Conely, owner and operator of Conely Speed

42

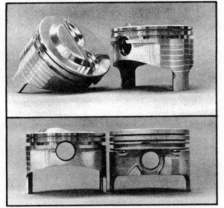

Special domed J.E. forged pistons (top) have only two ring grooves, are domed for high compression. Pin location (above) is higher than stock.

Walls of intake ports are milled away, replaced with welded plates to straighten and improve flow.

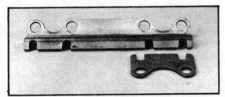

Special pushrod guide plates are required to help reposition rods after moving intake port walls.

Shop, and a Chevy man all the way. His shop is located in Brighton, Michigan, about a half-hour's drive northwest of Detroit and, oddly enough, quite close to the General Motors Proving Grounds.

By choice, Jack is a roundy-round racer . . . and a good one. He builds and drives his own cars, as well as building engines for himself and

many other East Coast and Midwestern racers. He is a one-man racing effort whose personal racing experiences have carried him as far as the Indianapolis 500 in an attempt to compete against the heavily sponsored, multi-million-dollar teams. But Conely's real love is racing his Super Modified, one of those narrow, tubular, open-wheeled cars with a minimum of sheet metal covering and an unlimited engine. It was for the Super Modifieds that Conely got into his extensive small-block development program. The result, a rash of broken lap records wherever the car is run—even against competition like Offys, Fords and big-block Chevys. No one can believe the power produced by the small-block engine, and few are willing to believe that Conely's engines could possibly have as large a displacement as the rumors claim. But they do.

Our first knowledge of Conely came from a Chevrolet engineer who mentioned the 454-inch small-blocks. That was impressive enough until Conely himself told us that he had built a pair of 482-inchers for a customer. But 454's are all Jack personally needs to dominate the Super Modified circuit in the northeastern United States. The engines are completely reliable and produce more than enough power to win consistently, much to the embarrassment of many big-block Chevy owners. Now, with the revision of drag racing's Pro Stock rules to include the compact cars and small-block engines, Jack is looking forward to lending some of his ability and experience to drag racing. Current plans call for some dyno work on carbureted small-block combinations suitable for Pro Stock and Modified Production classes to back up his knowledge of Super Modified-type injected motors that are ideally suited to Gas and Altered classes.

The engines that Jack builds for himself have a 454-cubic-inch displacement and, like all the large displacement small-blocks he builds, are based on the relatively new 400-cubic-inch cylinder block. For the 454-inch displacement, the stock 4-1/8 (4.125) inch bore is enlarged to 4-3/16 (4.1875) inches, an increase that has proven very acceptable in racing engines. For the larger engines such as the 482-cubic-inch version, the bore must be enlarged to 4.250 inches. Conely warns, however, that only *good* castings will accept a 4.250-inch bore. He suggests checking the cylinder walls of the casting with a dial indicator to determine the amount of core shift. If there is more than a .030-inch shift, the .125-inch overbore should not be

Hand-ground smooth radius helps prevent main web cracks, and notches are for rod clearance.

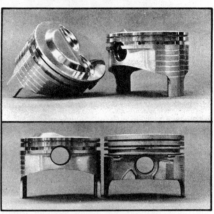

Special domed J.E. forged pistons (top) have only two ring grooves, are domed for high compression. Pin location (above) is higher than stock.

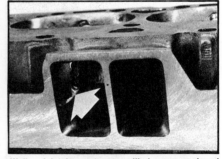

Walls of intake ports are milled away, replaced with welded plates to straighten and improve flow.

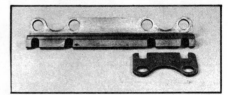

Special pushrod guide plates are required to help reposition rods after moving intake port walls.

attempted. If the shift is under .030 inch, the boring bar should be adjusted to compensate. As a rule of thumb, a properly done 4.250-inch-bore block will have a finished cylinder wall thickness of .110 inch.

Jack handcuts a 3/16-1/4-inch radius on the main webs at the point

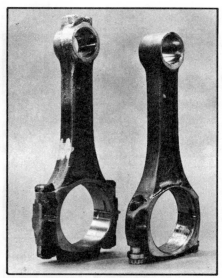

Race-ready connecting rod (right) is made from a selected, stock, 427-454 big-block rod (left).

Connecting-rod cap bosses are machined down for clearance, grooved for added strength (right).

Stock boss on small end of rod (left) must be cut off for inside piston clearance, oil hole added.

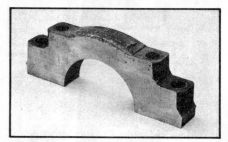

Milling side surfaces of main bearing caps makes visual detection of cracks easier, can save engine.

where the webs meet the cylinder banks (see photo). This radius removes the stock three-angle cut that the factory uses that often becomes the starting point for main web cracks. The sides of the main caps are milled to make visual detection of cracks easier during assembly and maintenance of the engine. The increased crankshaft throw also makes it necessary to grind notches at the

also reshaped around the bolt holes for cylinder-block clearance. The reinforcing pad across the bottom of the rod cap is machined down slightly for reduction of weight and improved clearance, and a radius is milled across the pad for increased rigidity (see photo). The stock rod bolts are replaced with special 7/16-inch, 4340 steel bolts. The forging marks are removed from the sides of the rods, and the small ends are radiused for weight reduction and interior piston clearance. An oil hole is also drilled in the rod's small end for improved lubrication to the floating piston pin. Finally, the entire rod is shot-peened for fatigue resistance.

Since there aren't any stock pistons available for the bore/stroke combinations Conely uses, he relies on custom forgings supplied by J E Pistons in Monterey Park, California. The combination of the long stroke and long rods places the pin hole unusually high in the forging, but this is beneficial in controlling the piston as it moves up and down in the cylinder. Only two piston rings are used: a single 1/16-inch dykes compression ring; and a 1/8-inch oil ring. The high pin height requires that the oil ring pass across the pin hole. Locating proper rings was also something of a problem, so Jack machines his own from moly castings supplied by TRW (chrome rings are used for better abrasion resistance in engines that are run on dirt tracks). The full-floating piston pins are special tapered items supplied by J E in a .990-inch diameter and a stock 427 big-block Chevy length. The pins are held in place by .072-inch-thick Spirolok retainers. With the gasolines now available, Jack usually settles for a maximum true compression ratio of 11.5:1.

To handle the large displacements, considerable work is done to the small-block cylinder heads. Dyno testing has shown an increase of 15 horsepower for the angle plug heads compared to heads with straight spark plug holes (both heads having the same chamber volume).

Conely's shop performs quite a bit of work on the ports beyond the usual porting and polishing. A mill is used to cut away the walls of the intake ports near the intake manifold surface (see photo). Iron plates are then welded into the head castings to replace the intake port walls, but the new plates are positioned so that the ports are effectively made larger and straighter. The new walls of the ports are moved enough so that they obstruct the stock intake pushrod guide holes, therefore the guide holes are slotted so that the pushrods can be moved slightly. The slotting also helps oil drainback to the bottom of the cylinder bores for rod clearance. Conely considers it an "absolute must" to O-ring the large-bore cylinder blocks.

As you might imagine, the crankshaft is a very non-stock part. Conely uses Moldex cranks exclusively, each one being completely machined from a billet of certified 4340 aircraft-quality steel, and each costing about $600. The 454's have a finished stroke of 4-1/8 inches, while the 482's go out to a full 4-1/4 inches. The Moldex cranks are completely crossdrilled and tufftrided, and have a 1/8-inch radius ground into the crank pins. No center counterweights are used. Balancing is accomplished by the installation of pieces of extremely heavy and expensive Mallory metal, since the cheaper and more common method of welding weight to the counterweights only adds to the crankshaft's clearance problems. The mains are ground to 2.648 inches; the throws are ground to 2.199 inches.

It's only fitting that a 454 should use 454 connecting rods, so Jack begins with selected, high-performance 454 big-block connecting rods. These forged-steel big-block rods are over one-half inch longer (center-to-center) than stock 400-inch small-block rods, and .435-inch longer than high-performance 302-350 rods. The long crankshaft stroke requires that a lot of material be removed from the big end of the

The amount the pushrods are offset is obvious when rocker arms are installed.

rod in the area of the bolt holes for camshaft clearance. The rod cap is cam valley. Offset buttons are also required in the tops of the intake valve lifters to help compensate for the pushrods, as are special offset guide plates which Conely manufactures. The whole thing becomes very obvious when the complete head is seen on an engine with the rocker arms in place and the valve cover

Offset lifter buttons (left) help locate pushrods moved during intake port work.

Finished combustion chamber shows some unshrouding and relative valve sizes.

removed. The exhaust rocker arms remain in their straight up/down position, while the intake rockers are canted at an angle (see photo).

Surprisingly, Jack uses smaller valves than most people would suspect in an engine of the size he runs. The intake valves range between 1-15/16 and 2 inches, smaller than stock 302 valves. The exhausts have a diameter of 1-11/16 inches. Conely has tried just about any valve combination you can name, including the tuliped MoPar hemi-style valves, and has settled for the above combination. He admits that the intake and exhaust valve pockets in the pistons and knowing how to unshroud the valve seats have a lot to do with making the small-block breathe. In any installation using the 400 cylinder block, steam vent holes

must be drilled in the heads to match the stock vent holes in the block between the siamesed cylinders.

There are very few people in the country who have done as much development on the small-block Chevy cylinder head as Conely. Besides all the unique valve combinations he has tried, he was working with open-chamber small-block heads as far back as ten years ago, and has experimented with canted-*valve* small-block heads.

Every Chevy enthusiast has heard of the legendary aluminum small-block heads—heard of them, but never seen any. Jack runs a set of them on his Super Modified engine. The best part is that the set he runs isn't his only set—he has lots of them, and they can be bought from him if you really want them or need them badly enough. Current plans call for limited availability of aluminum canted-valve (not just canted-plug, canted-*valve*) heads produced from his stock of in-line valve aluminum heads. The canted-valve heads produce a horsepower increase above 4000 rpm.

Jack's camshaft selections are based on his circle-track background. He uses Crower cams exclusively, most of them being roller tappet grinds. His favorite is a special 648-R grind cam (not listed in Crower's catalogue) that they grind for his large-displacement engines. It's a dual-pattern cam having a 320-degree intake duration and a 328-degree exhaust duration. The intake and exhaust lifts are .610 and .620 inch, respectively. Jack also uses Crower's roller lifters, retainers, pushrods and rev-kits.

The valve springs are special items Conely has produced from chrome-vanadium wire. The springs are a three-piece design (outer, inner, damper) and feature a .020-inch interference fit. The spring ends are also shaped to prevent them from gouging the retainers and possibly releasing aluminum chips into the oil. Conely guarantees the springs for life against breakage or the loss of more than five pounds of tension.

Since Jack runs his long-stroke engines in the 7500rpm range, he has given the lubrication system much work. The heart of the system is a big-block Chevy oil pump, originally designed for the ZL-1/427. This particular pump has longer gears (1.3 inches overall) than the small-block or standard big-block oil pumps for greater capacity, and Jack makes several modifications for use in his racing engines. The pump's slotted drive shaft is pressed .170-inch deeper into the gear. This insures that the distributor will have adequate clearance to seat properly when placed in the top of the engine. The burrs are removed from the

teeth of the pump's gears with a die grinder, and slots are cut in the body casting and cover with an end mill to prevent cavitation of the oil supply and the possibility of pumping only air. The cover is installed with a .0025-.003-inch clearance between it and the gears. Conely stocks the already modified ZL-1 pumps, selling them for about $35. The windage tray must be reworked to clear the body of the larger big-block pump. Jack also cuts slots in the windage tray for increased oil drainback. The slots are located to take advantage of the direction of rotation of the crankshaft, using the wind from the crank to force the oil out of the tray and back into the pan.

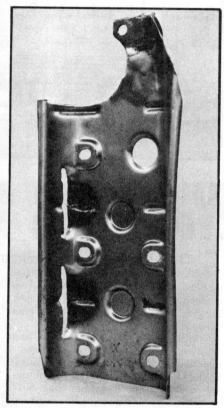

Small-block windage tray must be modified to clear the ZL-1/427 big-block oil pump.

Conely details his engines with such niceties as a Mallory magneto and Crower port injectors. He also uses rare, Chevy-built aluminum, small-block water pumps, which he sells for about $25.

On the dyno, the injected 454-inch small-blocks produce over 600 horsepower at 6800 rpm. That's good power in anyone's book. But when you consider that a small-block weighs about 150 pounds less than a comparable big-block Chevy engine, that's like being handed even more free power. Power to make people believe in the small-block.

illustration: John Jodauga

MOTOR BY ISKENDERIAN

The Hot Rod/Lee Eliminator Nova gets a 400-horsepower engine by Ed Iskenderian

By Steve Kelly ■ Building a race engine is usually a matter of relying on a certain set of known values. The engine is to be used only in a preordained environment, at a given rpm range, and for a specific amount of time. A street-operated engine is more complex. There is usually a performance standard set forth, but the rpm range can't be forecast, and the length of operating time can range from five minutes to five hours. Luckily, the men behind assembling the F.D.I. (Lee Eliminator) Chevy Nova 350 engine were cognizant of this, realizing that when the key was first turned on our giveaway Nova, it might not be turned off for quite a long period of time. Having had many years of experience in putting together both race engines and street engines, in addition to those doing double duty, Ed Iskenderian became our most logical choice for the man to supervise the construction and assembly of the Lee Eliminator Super Street Chevy 350 engine.

First thing Isky's men did was take the engine out and run it on their dyno. This showed the stock motor was delivering 216 horsepower at 4500 rpm.

The 8.5:1 compression ratio heads were traded for a set of 1970 model LT-1 Chevy heads. Chevrolet parts No. for the '70 vintage LT-1 head is 3987376. The intake valves are listed under No. 3849814, and the exhaust parts No. is 3849818. Combustion chamber displacement should not exceed 70 cubic centimeters. Just so you don't get the idea this was a bolt-on swap (although it can be), we left the new heads with Larry Ofria at Valley Head Service in Tarzana, California. Larry applied Valley's well-known "Street Master" head rework service. These LT-1 cylinder heads have 2⅛-inch intake valves and 1⅝-inch exhausts, so there's plenty of horsepower to be derived from a slight rework. Valley Head's rework for their "Street Master" application includes a total rework of all the *functional* parts of a cylinder head.

Along with checking the heads for surface smoothness, Valley Head finished the rework job by doing the "Marathon" valve treatment. This means a three-angle seat, in conjunction with flow-bench-proved seat angle and a back-cut angle on valves. The seats are ground to

Phil Weiand and Ed Iskenderian discuss the finer points of assembling the small-block street Chevy engine.

plus-or-minus .0005-inch tolerance, and valves are checked to within .001-inch total indicator runout reading.

Atop the nicely reworked heads, we chose to add a Weiand Exterminator single-four-barrel intake manifold. This is an intake setup we haven't paid as close attention to as we should have. It complements the 780-cfm double-pump-

MOTOR BY ISKENDERIAN

er four-barrel Holley carburetor and Iskenderian hydraulic cam perfectly. The camshaft used in this small-block is an Isky 210-HY hydraulic, better known as a "280 Hydraulic." It has .440-inch lift and appropriates good power between 2500 and 6500 rpm, making it nearly ideal for use with our Turbo-transmissioned Nova. Valve springs (Isky No. 6005) have 130 pounds seat pressure and are used in conjunction with Iskenderian needle bearings, aluminum rockers (No. 204) and No. 607-AL red anodized aluminum retainers. The split-lock valve locks are Isky parts No. VI-32, valve guides are conventional Perfect Circle type, and the pushrods used are chrome moly bottom and hardened (heat-treated) upper end from Isky, listed under parts No. 203-HG.

Naturally, our engine beginning life as an 8.5:1 engine means that if we are to register more than just a passing glance on the horsepower scale, the small-block Chevy will need more horsepower, and an increase in compression ratio transfers directly into horsepower. Besides swapping for a better (and more efficient) set of cylinder heads, we opted for a better set of pistons. Nick Arias delivered a set of

his Speed Masters to the Isky facility, grooved and ready to accept our Perfect Circle rings. The Arias pistons have a .006-inch skirt clearance, and when at full height within the combustion chamber, Arias' pistons displace 10.75:1 (approx.) compression. The $\frac{1}{16}$-inch top ring is molybdenum, while the second ring is durable, ductile iron. Iskenderian retained the stock ductile steel (cast) crank and drop-forged rods, but some insurance was provided when the crankshaft was forwarded to the Crank Shop in Inglewood for indexing. It was found that the crank was almost perfectly balanced, although each throw was .080-inch short of the established spec. This means the engine actually measures 342 cubic inches.

Iskenderian's men checked out the rods, using a relatively simple operation. They checked the center-to-center distance of each connecting rod on a jig-bore. The lead screw precision of the Moore jig-bore enables Iskenderian to pinpoint as close as a .0001-inch center-to-center tolerance. Iskenderian checks the align-bore of the crank by inserting a bar, sized for a main bearing journal *without* bearings in place, and they also use this to check

deck height. The tolerance of the deck height for our engine came to a maximum of .0008-inch.

Installation procedures required the use of some quality bearings. The ones used here were standard-size Clevite bearings. These bearings are standard in every way save for the bottom half of each main bearing. We asked for, and received, from our NAPA dealer, a set of Clevites with .0005-inch additional clearance on the bottom "shell."

Final assembly at Iskenderian's motor-making factory found our 350 (342 c.i.) engine going together using the aforementioned parts, all sealed tightly with Victor gaskets. The unique Victor intake manifold gasket(s) is made of Teflon, and can be used over and over again.

The outcome of all this engine-building showed up well on the Iskenderian dyno. The stock factory cam (hydraulic) is good for 5500-rpm engine speeds before the valves go into limbo. And as mentioned earlier, the best stock horsepower registered was 216 at 4500 rpm. Following some methodical work by the wizards at Iskenderian (their methods are now revealed to you), and a fair investment of money, the F.D.I. Nova has a 342-cubic-inch small-block Chevy capable of delivering over 425 horsepower in street form. ■ ■

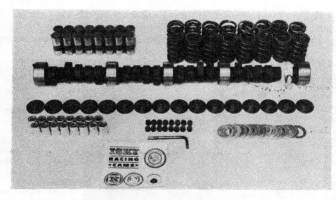

FAR LEFT — Isky hydraulic cam and valve kit are part of key to engine's potent dyno readings and smoothness.

LEFT — Valley Head Service applied the "Street Master" job to our LT-1-type heads. Flow is great, quality is excellent.

BELOW — Arias forged-aluminum high-dome pistons were fitted with Perfect Circle "moly top" rings. Connecting rods and crankshaft were checked for size and tolerance by the Crank Shop. Assembly made use of Clevite bearings.

BELOW — Valley Head put new seat angles on valves.
BELOW RIGHT — The Weiand Exterminator 4-bbl intake manifold was topped with a Holley 750-cfm double pumper. Combination is near-perfect throughout rpm range.

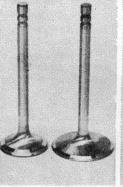

HOW TO TUNE: THE SMALL-BLOCK CHEVY

With this handy *CC* guide, even your car can carry a tune

With all the ballyhoo over how to stretch this or save that during the present gasoline shortage, one fact stands out from the rest as most vital to an efficient running vehicle—the common, ordinary tune-up.

Keeping our cars in constant tune is beneficial in many ways. An engine that operates smoothly and efficiently emits less pollutants, gets better mileage and stands a greater chance of lasting longer than one suffering from neglect. But before beating down your mechanic's door for an appointment, consider the possibility of doing the job yourself. It requires only a basic knowledge of things automotive, and the money you save alone will be worth the effort.

Let's examine our objective. First, what is a tune-up and how often need it be performed? A tune-up is basically a means of preventive maintenance; fixing or replacing a part in the engine compartment be-fore it has a chance to malfunction. The frequency depends largely on the vehicle and driving conditions, but every 12,000 miles or so is re-garded as an adequate interval. Tune-ups are as varied as the people who perform them. To our knowl-edge, the nomenclature extends to "minimum," "normal," "minor" and "major" tune-ups which, when bro-ken down, will give you an insight into what we're trying to accomplish here.

A "minimum" tune-up would entail cleaning the sparkplugs, filing the ig-nition points square and setting initial distributor timing. The benefits of cleaning the plugs and filing the points are doubtful at best. Setting the timing alone is a good move, mainly because the point contacts undergo normal wear, which eventu-ally retards initial timing. We suggest exchanging the plugs and points with fresh parts rather than attempting any cleaning process on your own.

The "normal" tune-up (the one we're basing this article on) amounts to replacing the plugs, points and condenser setting the timing, adjust-ing the carburetor's idle speed and mixture, and visually inspecting ev-erything under the hood.

Having the right tools helps a bunch. A bent box wrench is ideal for distributor hold down bolt.

GM distributors have dwell adjustment allowing for point setting with motor idling. Use Allen wrench to run screw in until engine stumbles, back off a full turn, then go back in a half turn.

Visual check should include cap and rotor for carbon tracks—a sign of dirt or moisture leading to possible short.

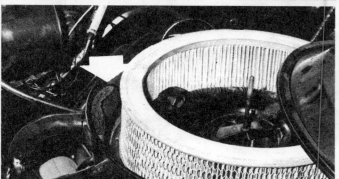

Air filter access is obvious, but check vent filter (arrow) for cleanliness and replace if necessary.

HOW TO TUNE

A complete "minor" tune-up might better be called an "electrical" tuning, because it generally involves the use of an oscilloscope and distributor machine. In addition to those items, the carburetor is treated to a chemical cleaning (in lieu of removal and rebuilding) and the following are checked: cranking voltage; vacuum and centrifugal advance; heat riser and/or air cleaner valve; PCV valve, carburetor choke and fast idle circuits; spark controls; battery terminals; all air, fuel and oil filters; compression or cylinder leakage test; and finally a road test.

A "major" tuning includes all of the above plus rebuilding the carburetor.

Other areas that should fall under your scrutiny are the carburetor and

HOW TO INSTALL POINTS

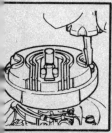
The following series of drawings, courtesy of Delco-Remy Division of General Motors, shows how to install points in several different distributors. A large Delco rotor is removed by taking out the two screws.

2. Removal of other types of rotors is accomplished by pulling up.

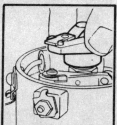
3. To install the type rotor that is shown, push it down over the distributor shaft. Do not press on rotor spring, if one is present. Make sure rotor is pushed all the way down to the shaft shoulder.

4. Note the locators on some types of rotors that correspond to the locating holes in the distributor weight base. When reassembling rotors of this type, the locators must match holes in the weight base for proper fit and for rotor tip location.

5. To remove the contact point set on the external adjustment type distributor, first note the lead arrangements in order that replacement may be properly made without interference with the cam, points or rotor. Then loosen screw and remove leads from the terminal as shown.

6. Loosen screws that hold contact point assembly to breaker plate.

7. Then remove points. Note locating holes in base of contact point set that fits over locating protrusion on breaker plate.

8. On other types of distributors, the nut on the primary terminal must be loosened to release the contact spring and the current-carrying member before removing the contact points. Here again the lead arrangement must be noted.

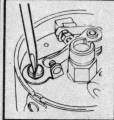
9. Then remove the one screw that holds the base of the contact point set to breaker plate.

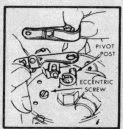
10. Lift up on the point set to remove it from the eccentric adjusting screw and pivot post.

11. On other types of distributors, the leads must be loosened from the contact point set as shown. Leads should be removed from the terminal after their relative positions have been noted.

12. Remove the two screws holding the base of point set to the breaker plate.

13. Remove point set from the distributor breaker plate. Note that condenser bracket is first removed to remove condenser. Note the locating tangs in the bracket that are used for properly locating the condenser.

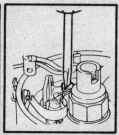
14. Still another type of distributor has its leads attached as shown. These must be removed by loosening the nut at the primary terminal.

15. Remove the base hold-down screw from the breaker plate.

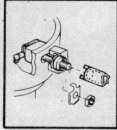
16. Then pull up to remove the contact point set from eccentric adjusting screw and pivot post

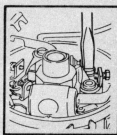
17. Another arrangement of the primary terminal is illustrated. To release the contact point spring and leads, a special tool must be used to remove the primary terminal nut.

18. Then remove all hold-down screws from contact point set base. Lift out to remove the points from the distributor.

19. After leads are removed from the primary terminal, loosen screw attaching condenser bracket to breaker plate to remove condenser. Note the locating tangs in the bracket that are used for properly locating the condenser.

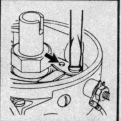
20. Other types of condensers have only one locating hole in the mounting bracket.

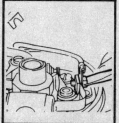
21. On those distributors containing two sets of breaker points, note lead arrangements and loosen primary terminal leads from each set.

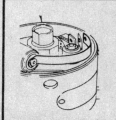
22. Some types of condensers are connected to the primary terminal by a copper strap which must be released before the condenser can be removed.

23. To aid in obtaining proper replacement parts, refer to the distributor model number which is located on the breaker plate of some distributors.

24. On other distributors, the model number may be found either on the tag on the side of the housing or on a band fastened around the housing.

HOW TO TUNE

intake manifold bolts, distributor hold-down, its cap and wiring. You may incorporate all or part of these items into your tune-up; we're simply presenting them for your enlightenment.

With all this in mind, let's embark on a new monthly feature wherein *CAR CRAFT* shows how to maintain your own vehicle. Our first installment deals with the small-block Chevrolet, easily the most abundant engine on the road today. It would be in your favor to have on hand a shop manual or Petersen's "How To Tune Your Car," an invaluable bit of information for the do-it-yourselfer. ℂ

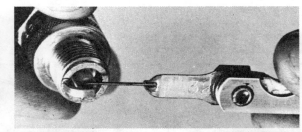

FIRING ORDER 1-8-4-3-6-5-7-2

The firing order for all Chevy small-block engines is 1, 8, 4, 3, 6, 5, 7, 2. The left bank cylinder numbers are 1, 3, 5, 7; and the right are 2, 4, 6, 8. When timing the engine be sure to use the #1 cylinder. The timing tabs are shown at right. Clean and mark them with chalk or paint so that it is easier to read the degree marks with a timing light.

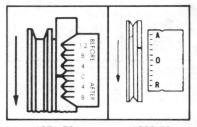

1971-72   1968-70
Each space is 2°

After you've chosen a heat range similar to stock specs, use an item like this wire gauge to gap the plugs at .032.

Swivel head ratchet saves skinned hands when trying to reach a well-hidden plug. Some might have to use hex-head socket and open-end wrench.

Smog valves (PCV) should be replaced if clogged when removed and shaken.

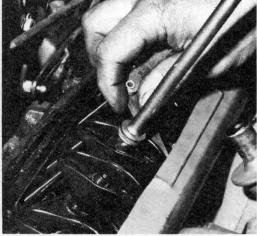

Noisy valves need adjusting. Use feeler gauge to measure gap between rocker arm and valve tip. Turn engine by hand to close valves (engine can be running if cut valve cover is used to catch oil runoff). Chevy solid lifter cams like .030 on both the intakes and exhausts. Hydraulic cam settings are zero lash. With engine running, tighten juice lifters until noise barely goes away, plus one full turn.

Idle mixture screws (shown here on Rochester 4MV) regulate low-speed air requirement. Begin adjustment by cranking screws all the way in and then backing them off a turn and a half, or until you've achieved smoothest idle. If idle is smooth but high, turn down idle speed screw next to throttle linkage.

Holley screws (one on either side of primary metering plate) are adjusted same as Q-Jet: all the way in and 1½ turns out, or until smooth idle is attained.

A NEW HEAD FOR THE MOUSE

Chevy's new small-block cylinder head features seven major improvements and substantial horsepower gains

Text & photos by Ray Casner ▪ You'd think that after nearly two decades of useful and productive life, the design of the small-block Chevy engine would be just about used up. But such is not the case. Ask any speed shop owner and he'll tell you that the majority of his speed equipment sales are made to small-block Chevy owners. What is it that has kept the little engine alive and popular for the past 20 years? Aside from some of its more obvious features, like good basic design, excellent power potential and light weight, the small-block Chevy has the distinct advantage of being backed up by a little-known group of "checked-out" factory engineers who continue to develop new low-cost, high-quality performance pieces each and every year. And they've done it again.

This time, the guys at the Chevrolet Engineering Center (whose group is known as "Product Promotion Engineering") have outdone themselves with a newly designed, off-road cylinder head that will probably be one of the hottest-selling items since sliced bread. What they've done, essentially, is to provide the racing public with a new cylinder head that has the most desirable "as-cast" port configurations that could possibly be incorporated into existing manufacturing techniques, both casting and machining. Also, they've added metal to a number of strategic areas where the present casting was too thin for current aftermarket modifications, and they have eliminated

the heat crossover that disrupted flow in the one exhaust port (where welding was formerly required as a cure).

Before getting into specifics on the improved head, we should point out that an entirely new method of development was used to yield its final design. In the past, a new cylinder head such as this would have been designed and drawn (or put into blueprint form) in "theory" *only*. Then the foundry would have made a prototype from the blueprint for testing. If it was unsatisfactory, they would have had to repeat the entire procedure until the desired results were obtained. And as critical as port shape is to air flow, the optimum design could have conceivably taken years to finalize. In addition, the costs incurred by the long trial-and-error procedure could have been astronomical. As a result, the normal method was reversed. A current casting was modified, by hand, to produce a mock-up version of the final product *before* drawing the blueprints. Once finalized, molds of the individual ports were taken so they could be accurately measured and incorporated into the blueprints from which the foundry made the production prototype. That way, they knew the end result would be exactly the way it was supposed to be.

When the current angle-plug head (Chevy part No. 3965742) was introduced in 1970, with its superior plug location for faster flame travel and resultant power increases, it soon became the standard for small-block racing engines. But this latest

design, carrying Chevy part No. 340292, features no less than *seven* (count 'em) major refinements. They are (1) improved inlet port, (2) improved exhaust port, (3) elimination of heat-crossover port, (4) removal of the (cast) pushrod guides, (5) unshrouding around one side of the spark plug, (6) more metal around the valve spring pockets and (7) increased size of the rocker arm stud bosses.

New technology in the areas of cam timing, induction systems, flow bench work, etc., had shown a need for improved flow in the intake port, so this is where the majority of the flow increases were made. And to improve upon a port that had already been proven very successful was no easy task. To do it, many hours were spent on and off the flow bench, in conjunction with removing material from some areas of the port and adding it to others with Devcon (an epoxy-based material). The differences between the old and the new ports are quite obvious in the accompanying cutaway photos and drawings. Also, two of the charts reveal the increased flow and cross-sectional area of the new port, as compared to the old.

Exhaust flow was improved also, but not to as great an extent as the intake. This was due, in part, to previous dyno work that had shown little power difference in the 6000-to-8000-rpm range (where most small-blocks "work out") between the stock exhaust port and those of several known porters. This is not to say that exhaust flow cannot be improved by raising the port, welding or some of the other more exotic techniques. It's just that any change of this magnitude would not have fallen within the confines of the existing casting, nor would it have been compatible with the current exhaust systems (both factory and aftermarket). As shown in the photos and illustrations, the exhaust port received only subtle changes, but they *did* increase potential flow.

Because the new head features the elimination of the heat-crossover port used to warm the base of the carburetor during cold warm-ups, it should not be used on the street, where increased emissions will result from cold-start conditions. Thus it has been termed an "off-road" part by Chevrolet. But the elimination of heat to the carburetor was not the primary reason for its removal. Since it entered one of the exhaust ports, the passage also disrupted flow in that port by causing unwanted turbulence and unevenness between it and the others. Therefore, the new head benefits flow in yet another significant way.

While not having any substantial advantage in regard to performance, the removal of the cast pushrod guides *does* account for a slight reduction in weight and increased flow of the returning oil. As shown in the photos, the amount of metal surrounding these guide holes was significant, but highly unnecessary when the late-style, bolt-on pushrod guide plates are used.

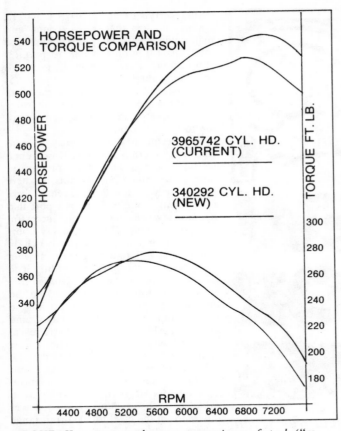

HORSEPOWER AND TORQUE COMPARISON

3965742 CYL. HD. (CURRENT)

340292 CYL. HD. (NEW)

HORSEPOWER — TORQUE FT. LB.

RPM: 4400 4800 5200 5600 6000 6400 6800 7200

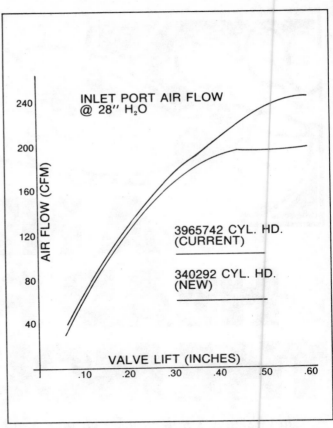

INLET PORT AIR FLOW @ 28″ H$_2$O

AIR FLOW (CFM)

3965742 CYL. HD. (CURRENT)

340292 CYL. HD. (NEW)

VALVE LIFT (INCHES): .10 .20 .30 .40 .50 .60

ABOVE—Horsepower and torque comparisons of stock ("as-cast") heads were performed on a 302-inch Formula 5000 engine with fuel injection, cam, pistons, headers, etc.

ABOVE—Air flow in the inlet port was vastly improved. Note especially the flow increase above .45-inch valve lift, where the old intake port seemed to level off.

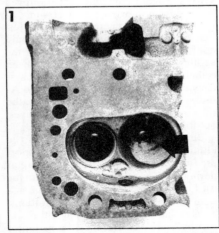

LEFT & BELOW—This sequence shows the "backwards" development process used to produce the new head (see text). (1) This is the casting that was used on the flow bench for port development. Arrow shows Devcon added to port. (2) This mold was then taken, using a pliable substance for easy removal. (3) This fixture was then used to cast a two-piece female mold that established a parting line for the foundry. (4) Here are the two halves of the female mold and another male mold of the port showing the parting line. (5) The final step was to cast a "hard" mold in the two-piece female mold, then section it so its measurements could be drawn into blueprints.

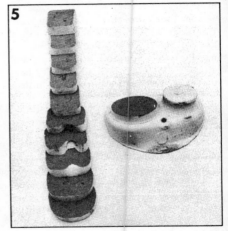

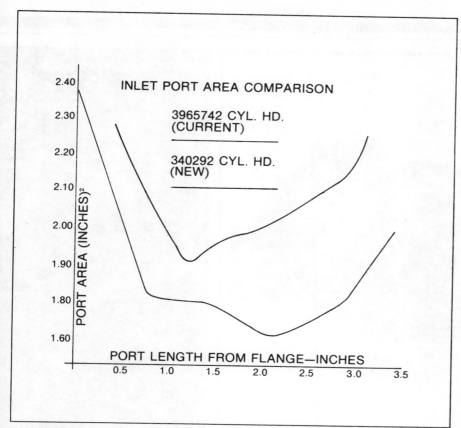

INLET PORT AREA COMPARISON

3965742 CYL. HD.
(CURRENT)

340292 CYL. HD.
(NEW)

PORT AREA (INCHES)^2

PORT LENGTH FROM FLANGE—INCHES

ABOVE—This graph shows how much bigger the new intake port really is. The initial reduction in port size, at left, is required to clear the intake pushrods.

ABOVE—Here we see the unshrouding of the spark plug and the void where the heat crossover used to be. BELOW—Arrows indicate how the pushrod area on the new head (right) differs from the old. The spring pockets on the new head were machined to show how big they could be made, but they won't come that way stock.

The trimming of the metal from the combustion chamber around one side of the spark plug was done primarily for ease of machining, although it did result in other racer benefits. On the current angle-plug heads, the surface in the chamber where the spark-plug hole is located is not perpendicular to the tap that threads the hole. Therefore, a portion of the combustion chamber surface adjacent to the plug hole would sometimes break off unevenly and cause the demise of a tap. Additionally however, the exposed thread cuts sometimes caused hot spots in the chamber (resulting in preignition) and impeded flame travel as well. All these problems were solved by merely doing away with the metal (see photo).

The other two items in the previous list of seven were incorporated into the new casting to benefit those people who are not satisfied with the stock versions and wish to have them modified. Many an experienced head porter has struck water when enlarging the valve spring seats to accommodate larger springs for the latest high-lift cams. The Chevy engineers cured the problem once and for all by adding enough material around the spring seats so they could be safely enlarged to as big as 1.55 inches in diameter without even coming close to breaking through. And speaking of high lift, they also enlarged the rocker-stud bosses so the studs can be safely relocated .15-inch farther from the valve to accommodate the higher-lift (and stronger) 1.75:1 rat motor rockers. Additionally, a number of less significant changes were made to water cores (in both shape and size) and other key areas to allow current porting techniques to be employed where there would previously have been problems.

All things considered, the new head offers many improvements over its predecessors, while still maintaining the ability to accept all hardware that's used with the present casting, such as intake and exhaust manifolding, valvetrain components, gaskets, etc. Special credit should be given to Mr. V.W. Piggins (head of the Product Promotional Group), Herb Fishel (in charge of the project) and Ron Sperry (theoretical and design work) for their hard and dedicated work. And, as can be seen in the accompanying power chart, it was well worth the effort. On the engine tested, which is typical of those found in Formula 5000 road race cars with headers, cam, fuel injection, etc., a gain of more than 20 hp was realized at 7000 rpm, along with corresponding improvements throughout the rest of the rpm band as well. And that was a comparison between bone-stock production-line versions! As of this writing, the new heads will be available around the first of the year and will be comparable in price to the existing angle-plug versions (rumor has them at about $90). So what's next from the guys at Chevy? Who knows? But whatever it is, it's bound to be good. ■ ■

HEAVY-DUTY SMALL-BLOCK PARTS

350-c.i.d. short-block assembly, four-bolt main cap, mechanical lifter cam, crank, rods, 11:1 pistons, timing chain and gears, 370 hp	3966921
350 crank	3941184
11:1 pistons, pressed pin	3942541
Spirolox retainers	3946848
2.02-inch intake valve	3849814
1.60-inch exhaust valve	3849818
screw-in rocker studs	3973416
pushrod guide plates	3973418
heavy-duty valve springs	3927142
302 dampener	3947708
327 dampener	3817173
Z-28 oil pan	3974251
tray baffle	3927136
tray mounting studs	3960312
piston rings	3995664
street mechanical cam	3972178
street hydraulic cam	3896962
mechanical lifter	5232695
edge orifice hydraulic lifter	5231585
piddle valve lifter	5232695
pressed pin connecting rod	3973386
floating pin rod	3946841
⅜-inch rod bolt	3916399
⅜-inch rod nut	3866766
high-riser intake manifold	3972114
distributor	1111267
transistor ignition unit	3997782
magnetic pulse amplifier	3955511
coil	1115207
connector	2977253
harness assembly	6297688
wire assembly	8914473
terminal	2962572
flywheel	3991406
10.5-inch, 3100-lb pressure plate	6273958

THE MOUSE THAT LIVES

THE STARTING POINT TO BUILDING A BULLET PROOF SMALL-BLOCK CHEVY IS BEING ARMED WITH ALL THE HEAVY-DUTY PART NUMBERS/By John Thawley

The small-block Chevy is the most popular engine used by hot rodders. They're stuffed into roadsters, coupes, sedans, fad cars, trucks, campers and tractors, and flogged back and forth to work for thousands of miles in all kinds of conditions. The popularity of the little engine is just short of staggering. So many aftermarket parts are available that an engine could be built without using anything from Chevy except the block. That's the hard way to do it, of course, and certainly not the

most practical. Armed with the correct part numbers, anyone can gather up the right hardware for a bulletproof engine from the local Chevy dealer. More and more guys around the country are driving longer distances in early irons and discovering what racers have known for some time—the way to build a bulletproof small-block is to start with new stock Chevy parts and go from there.

So here, on paper, we'll round up the hardware and part numbers for a bulletproof small-block 350-c.i.d.

Chevy. Couple it to a 3 or 4-speed box, Powerglide or Turbo-Hydro, drop it into most any vehicle in your current or future stable and drive it!

If you prefer to limit your travels back and forth to the Chevy parts counter, the smart move is to take delivery on part number 3966921. This is the 350-c.i.d. short-block assembly centered around a four-bolt main-cap block fitted with a mechanical cam, large journal crank, heavy-duty rods, 11:1 pistons, timing chain and gears. This assembly is rated at

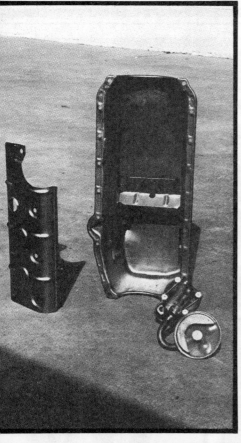

1. Chances are if you're currently running a stock pan on your small-block, this Z-28 pan and tray baffle setup will fit in the chassis with no problems. Tray can be used on any four-bolt main block. Z-28 oil pump is 3848907.

2. Don't despair if you have some two-bolt main blocks sitting around—they can be converted to four-bolt by use of a Milodon kit as has been done on this block. Check that degreed dampener.

3. Chevy has two hydraulic lifters. On the left is the piddle valve lifter; item on the right is the edge orifice unit recommended for high rpm engines. Either will work with any of the Chevy juice cams—just don't mix them within an engine.

4. Even all-out race engines rely on this high-capacity Chevy fuel pump which can be used on any small-block. The part number is 6415325.

5. The current 350s are equipped with super-low compression cast aluminum pistons which are dished and notched. They can be replaced with earlier 350 pistons supplied by Chevy or TRW.

370 horsepower—and it will produce that when the engine is completed with the rest of the "good guy" Chevy hardware we outline here.

To complete the assembly you'll need a set of heads, a distributor, intake manifold, oil pan, oil pump, front cover and water pump. So stocked, you'll be ahead of the game, unless you have a work bench stacked with Chevy parts. We'll assume from here on that the engine of your dreams will be purchased and assembled piece by piece, so the

rest of the article will deal with individual parts, not assemblies.

The bare 4-inch bore, four-bolt main block (large journal) goes by the part number 3970016. This block can also be used to build a 327-c.i.d., using crank 3914681, or a 302-c.i.d., using crank 3941176. These engines share the same 4-inch bore; the only difference is in the stroke which is the result of the various cranks.

We figure the plan for the guy on the street is the 350-c.i.d. since it

won't cost any more to build in the long run, and any time we can get some more inches for free, we'll take 'em. The exception to this rule is the 400-c.i.d. This is a good engine, but unless you get involved in mega-buck aftermarket hardware, it can be difficult to build a potent 400 inches. The engine is not as quick to rev as the smaller displacement engines, and is therefore most likely to come out second best in a run through the gears unless subjected to a considerable massage. Don't let us discour-

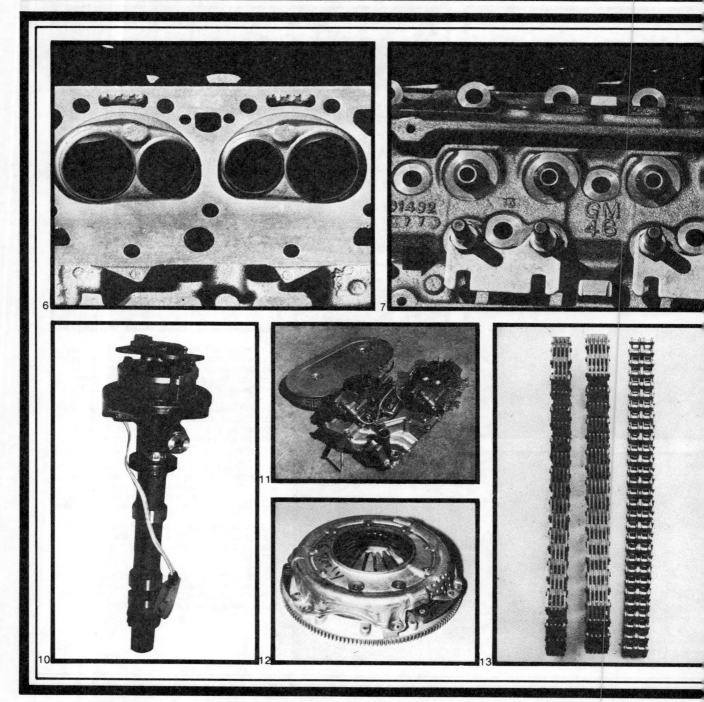

age you from picking up a 400-incher if you can find one in good condition for the right price. At that point the plan would be to install a very short duration aftermarket camshaft.

Due to the displacement, torque, horsepower and availability of low-cost hardware, most engine builders feel the 350-c.i.d. Chevy engine is probably the most versatile displacement to deal with for all-around use. If you do go the 350-c.i.d. route, you should know that the crank for this displacement is 3941184. Thanks to Chevy, the crank has already been balanced for use with their standard forged 11:1 pistons which bear the part number 3942541. This is a pressed pin piston and is entirely adequate for street use. However, if you must buy a set of pistons for our make-believe engine, check on the availability of 3959448. This is the same piston, only machined and equipped with a floating wrist pin. If you do come up with a set of these slugs, you'll have to have a set of Spirolox retainers, part number 3946848.

Cylinder heads are important in the horsepower end of building any engine. At the time of this writing, the trick head for building a small-block street engine would be the slant-plug unit with big valves. Intake valve size is 2.20 inches; exhaust valve is 1.60 inches. The head number is 336746—that's for a bare head. Valves can be found under 3849814 and 3949818 for intake and exhaust respectively. These heads are drilled and tapped

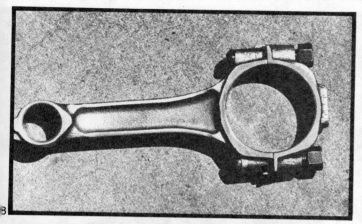

6. This is what you're looking for in the combustion chamber regardless of where you buy the heads. The intakes are 2.02-inch, exhausts are 1.60-inch.

7. All good heads have screw-in rocker studs and are fitted with the pushrod guide plates (arrow). Earlier heads with pressed-in studs can be converted to the screw-in type by milling stud bosses .250-inch.

8. Chevrolet can supply you with a heavy-duty rod setup for a floating pin or a shotpeened pressed-in pin for heavy-duty use.

9. The Chevy high-riser single 4-bbl aluminum intake manifold can be improved by a ¾-inch spacer between carb and manifold.

10. Hot tip for the budget builder is this magnetic-impulse plain-bearing distributor with tach drive (1111267).

11. Chevy used to offer this dual 4-bbl manifold for the 302 in '67 when Penske and Donohue had a lock on Trans Am.

12. This is the ultimate clutch and flywheel package available from Chevy for the small-block.

13. Chevy has three timing chains and matching gear sets available for the small-block.

14. The five long studs shown here are Chevy items needed to mount tray baffle along with tying down main bearing caps.

15. Most small-block Chevys can survive for a long time if the stock oil pump is used with a reworked pickup utilizing a ⅜-inch-diameter tube running from pump to pickup.

screw-in rocker studs (part number 3973416). Before clamping them down tightly in the head (with Loctite), put a set of the pushrod guide plates in place (3973418). Currently, the hot tip on heavy-duty valve springs for the small-block is 3927142.

There's always a question mark when guys get around to the crank dampener—maybe this will help. If you're building a 350-c.i.d., four-bolt main, large-diameter journal engine, then the Z-28/LT-1 dampener (3947712) is the item to use. For a four-bolt main, large-diameter journal engine of 302 inches, the harmonic dampener to use is 3947708. Late (large journal diameter) 327-c.i.d. engines get harmonic dampener 3817173. Any block using a crank dampener with the keyway and the TDC mark aligned should be accompanied by timing chain cover 3923290. On those dampeners not having the keyway and the timing mark aligned the cover to use is 3991433. This cover has no timing scale attached, so you'll take care of that with a 3991436 and attach it to the cover and block with two of the ¼-inch cap screws that hold the cover in place.

If the Z-28 oil pan will fit in your chassis, that's the one to use. The part number is 3974251. You can fit a tray baffle (3927136) into that pan if you'll use five special studs (3960312) that tie into the main bearing caps. This tray baffle is worth a couple of horsepower—even on a street machine since it keeps the

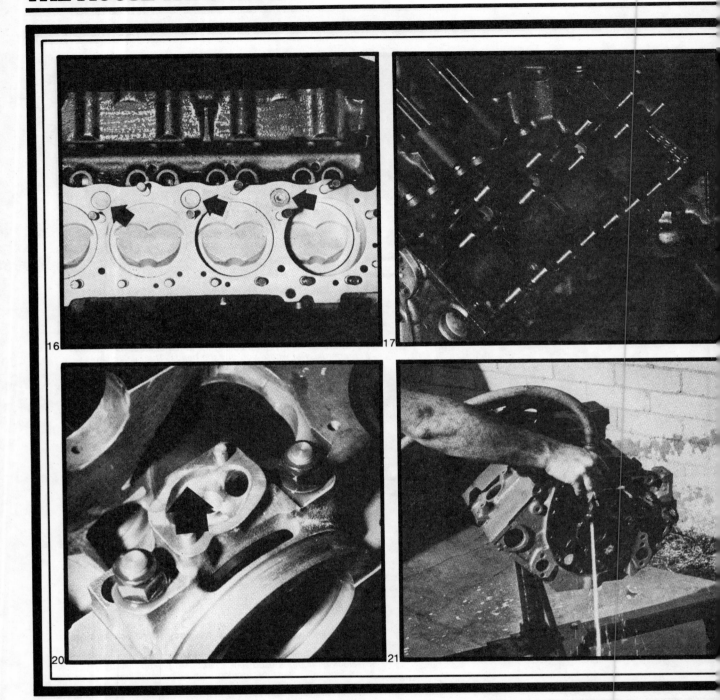

16

17

20

21

crank from whipping through that gurgling sea of oil.

For all around use, stock low-tension Chevy piston rings are hard to beat. Part number 3995664 is the one to get—that's for one piston.

There are a lot of ways to go in the camshaft department—and all have Chevy part numbers. We'll give you two choices to keep it simple. The cam used in the '70 and '71 Z-28 engine is a streetable mechanical cam, part number 3972178. Exhaust lift is .455-inch; intake lift is .434-inch. Duration is 314 on the ex-

haust cycle and 300 degrees for the intake valves. If you go this route or use any other mechanical cam, the correct lifter is 5231585. There is a hydraulic cam with .450 lift. That part number is 3896962. There are two mechanical lifters, and either will work well with any of the Chevy mechanical cams. For racing we'd pick the edge orifice lifter (5231585). The piddle valve lifter is found under 5232695.

There are two ways to fly on the connecting rods. Chevy offers one with a pressed-in pin and one with a

floating pin. The pressed-in pin item has been shotpeened at the factory in the area of the bolt and nut seats. That's 3973386. The floating pin item has not been shotpeened, but that's simple enough to do once the rods are in hand. The floating pin rod is 3946841. You'll need 16 each of 3916399, which is the ⅜-inch rod bolt, and also of 3866766, which is the rod nut.

For good low end response and a nice, smooth power curve right on up to 4500 rpm, you'll find the stock Z-28/LT-1 high-riser single 4-bbl

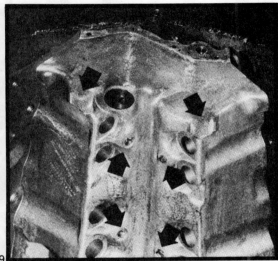

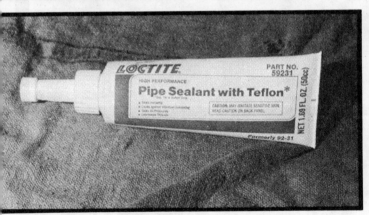

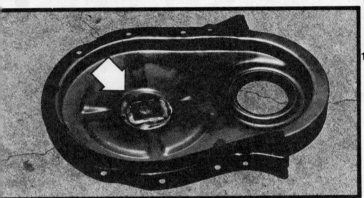

16. *Plugging the three large coolant holes in the deck surface of the block will even out the water flow in the block considerably and promote better cooling.*

17. *Using studs in the block for mounting the heads will pay off in an engine that is frequently torn down.*

18. *To ensure that the main caps have absolutely no lateral movement in the block, clamp the caps in place and then peen the adjacent block surface with a small punch until the cap is a snug fit.*

19. *A gentle deburring of the galley area promotes oil drain-back, while pieces of stainless steel screen epoxied into the block will prevent foreign items of any size from making it to the oil pan. Note also that the oil drain-back holes next to the cam have been plugged to eliminate the oil being whipped by the cam.*

20. *To aid oil flow when putting a small-block together, give a generous radius to that area of the main cap that mates with the stock oil pump.*

21. *When rebuilding a block, use plenty of soap and water for the final clean-out—after the block has been boiled out and machined—and dry with air hose and lint-free rags.*

22. *Here's a no-cost trick to keep the cam from walking forward in the block—which will change timing at the distributor. Braze a small pad on the inside of the timing chain cover to prevent the cam from moving any further.*

23. *This product by Loctite is the current ''hot tip'' for use on all screw-in fittings on a small-block Chevy.*

manifold is hard to beat, part number 3972144. It's a lot easier to overcarburet a small-block Chevy than most people realize. For street driving we'd have to give the nod to the 600-cfm Holley which bolts onto the Chevy manifold. You can pick up a pony or two if you install an accessory spacer plate (about ¾-inch thick) between the carb and manifold.

For a distributor, the hot tip is 1111267. This is a plain bearing item with tach drive and vacuum advance. To finish off the ignition system you'll need the Chevy transistor ignition unit (3997782) which includes the magnetic pulse amplifier (39955511), coil (1115207), connector (2977253), harness assembly (6297688), wire assembly (8901973) and terminal (2962572).

If you plan to buckle this engine to a Turbo-Hydro, then you won't have any use for the lightweight nodular iron flywheel (3991406) or the 3100-pound load, 10.5-inch clutch (3886066).

We fully realize that there will be a few of you who start out from scratch and build the engine that we've described, but if you keep this story around, you'll find that the part numbers will come in mighty handy if you decide to upgrade your present engine with new parts. For instance, with only the studs, tray baffle and Z-28 oil pan you can upgrade any four-bolt main small-block in a low-cost Saturday morning. Two weekends later, you might spring for a new cam. By the time you get around to a new set of heads, you'll be telling yourself you're about the best small-block builder around. No way—Chevy is!

350 *Street* BUILDUP

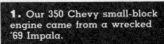

1. Our 350 Chevy small-block engine came from a wrecked '69 Impala.

2. All parts not involved in the machine work were removed before the engine was taken to Valley Head Service in Northridge, California.

3. After the block was thoroughly disassembled, it was hot-tanked to remove more than 10 years' worth of grit and grime.

HOW TO BUILD THE PERFECT ENGINE FOR YOUR CLASSIC CHEVY

TEXT & PHOTOS: BRUCE CALDWELL

There seems to be an endless list of reasons for building, owning, and having fun with the classic '55-'57 Chevrolet. One of the foremost "plus" features is the ease with which the drivetrain can be maintained or modified. The '55 Chevy was the first of millions of Chevrolet products to use the legendary small-block V8. Chevrolet wisely kept its various small-blocks very similar to the original design in the ensuing decades. So finding engine parts for your classic Chevy is easier than with any other collector's car.

Of all the various small-block configurations there is one that stands out from the rest: the 350-cubic-inch version that was first introduced in 1967. The 350 is readily available, reasonably priced, a snap to install in any '55-'57 Chevy, and capable of both good economy and very respectable performance.

The 350 Chevy small-block engine is what we term an ideal "fun engine." That is, it can be assembled with readily available aftermarket parts to yield a reliable engine capable of 20-mile-per-gallon highway mileage while still having plenty of power for that old-fashioned "kick in the pants" feeling.

The fun engine will deliver all the performance anyone but an all-out drag racer will ever need. A well-built 350 Chevy allows you to have all the fun of the Fifties and Sixties with the economy of the Eighties. The engine is just like your classic Chevy—the best of both worlds.

Our fun engine was built by the engine experts at Valley Head Service (19340 Londelius, Northridge, CA 91324, 213/993-7000). Valley Head Service is equipped to handle all types of standard and custom machine work as well as all phases of engine building, assembly, and dyno testing. For customers not fortunate to live near their bustling facility they also provide mail-order service ranging from work on customer's parts to complete, no-exchange, ready-to-run engines. A catalog detailing their parts and services is available for $3.

Follow along as we show you how to build the perfect engine for your classic Chevrolet.

Before you can build a fun engine you need to have the basic 350 engine, and there are several places to obtain one. If you are really bucks up, you can still buy a brand-new, in-the-crate 350 from Chevrolet. The prices are reasonable, but considering the millions of 350s around today and their great longevity, finding a good used 350 is no problem.

4. The crankshaft main saddles were checked to see if any align-boring would be needed. Before making any measurements, it is a good idea to touch up the mating surfaces with a honing stone.

5. The block was tapped to accept the new four-bolt main caps from the Valley Head Service four-bolt cap kit.

6. The align-boring process requires that the block be precisely located and completely level.

7. The crankshaft was checked with a micrometer prior to regrinding.

8. The block boring is a two step process. First the block was bored .025-inch on the boring bar.

9. The last .005-inch of the boring operation is performed on a Sunnen hone. A torque plate is used to simulate cylinder head loads on the block.

10. The block was decked to make sure all surfaces were exactly perpendicular to the cylinder bores.

11. All the connecting rods were rebuilt on a Sunnen rod rebuilding machine. They were also Magnafluxed to detect any flaws.

12. All moving parts were balanced. Rods are weighed on each end and then lightened to match the lightest ends.

13. The Speed Pro pistons were also weighed to determine the lightest one.

14. Excess weight on the rods is ground off the pads, which are designed for just that purpose.

15. Weight removal for the pistons is accomplished on a lathe.

16. The crankshaft was balanced on a special strobe light-equipped reciprocating balancer.

Wrecking yards are full of 350s, as are your local want ads. Wrecking yards know the value of these super popular engines and charge accordingly. Buying an engine laying behind some guy's garage may or may not be a good deal. Of course, the guy will always tell you that the engine ran "like a top," but then why did he dump it?

The best way to find an engine for rebuilding is to locate one that is still in a running car. This way you can check the engine for major defects. And it is possible to buy a damaged or badly ailing car with a good engine for little more than the cost of the engine alone. That is how we obtained the engine for this story. An ad in a local throwaway newspaper offered a crashed '69 Impala four-door sedan for $200. The engine had a little more than 100,000 miles on it and smoked slightly. It was as grimy as all get out, but it ran fine. Many other parts (including all the little linkage and miscellaneous hardware so vital to an engine swap) were salvaged before the battered hulk was sent to the scrap dealer.

After the engine was removed from the car, all the accessory items were removed. If the machine shop doesn't need a particular part, don't send it along. The only parts we sent to Valley Head Service were those needed for the rebuilding process. Since we knew we were going to add an aftermarket manifold and carburetor, even those parts were removed.

When the engine arrived at Valley Head Service it was completely disassembled and thoroughly hot-tanked. A couple trips through the hot-tank process were necessary to remove more than 10 years of dirt and grime.

After everything was good and clean, the engine was thoroughly mic'd and inspected. All the cylinder bores were checked for size and taper. The crankshaft was checked with a micrometer and found to be slightly out of round. This meant that a regrind and .010-inch-under bearing would be needed. The cylinders were in amazingly good condition for a 100,000-mile engine, so only a slight boring was necessary. The normal .030-inch bore job was all that was called for. The bore of the crank bearings was also checked. This is done with the main saddles torqued in place. Our engine wasn't bad, but it was slightly off so an align-boring was in order.

Careful inspection and conscientious use of precision measuring tools is vital to a good engine buildup. If you don't know where you stand before, during, and after machine work, you won't have a precision job. After the inspection, it is time for the actual machine work.

While the block of our 350 Chevy was being worked on, we decided to add some extra bottom end insurance. Our block, like most 350s, was just a two-bolt main block, not the more desirable, stronger four-bolt main version. Rather than spend the extra money and time needed to secure a four-bolt main block, we had Valley Head Service install one of their four-bolt main cap conversion kits. It is an easy matter to install the four-bolt main cap kit while the block machine work is being performed. The four-bolt kit must be installed prior to boring the block because all machine operations are referenced off the main bearing saddles. Should we ever decide to extract more horsepower from our engine, we know the bottom end is up to the task. In the meantime, there is the security and status that comes with the saying, "It's a four-bolt block."

The boring of a cylinder block is a two-step process. First the block is set up on a boring bar that locates the block off the main saddles so the bores are perpendicular to the crankshaft. Each bore was enlarged .025-inch on the boring bar with the final .005-inch boring, second, being performed on a Sunn'en CK-10 honing machine. Each Speed Pro piston was checked with a micrometer before honing to ensure the same piston-to-wall clearance for all cylinders. Valley Head Service does all honing operations with a torque plate on the block to simulate the loads imposed on the cylinders by the cylinder heads.

The block was then decked to make sure that the distance between the crankshaft centerline and the head surface or deck was the same at all corners of the block. The tolerance should be held to .001-inch. After the machine work is over, Valley Head Service again hot-tanks the block to remove honing oils and any debris that may have accumulated during the machine work.

After the block work, the crew at Valley Head Service went to work on the internal engine pieces. The crankshaft was checked and found to be out of round, so it was reground to accept .010-inch undersize Sealed Power bearings. The oil holes in the crank were chamfered with a hand-held grinder to improve oiling. The crank was also micropolished to remove the tiniest burrs.

The stock connecting rods were retained after Valley Head Service Magnafluxed them to check for any damage. The rods were bead-blasted clean and rebuilt. A Sunnen cap-and-rod grinder is used to make sure all contact surfaces are perfect and honed to an exact size, and the rods are put in an alignment fixture to make sure the rod pins are perpendicular to the center of the bore.

All the rods were weighed and balanced, each rod end being weighed separately. Both ends are matched to the lightest weight for that end. All reciprocating parts are balanced on Valley Head Service's Stewart-Warner balancing equipment.

Sealed Power cam bearings were installed in the block and new freeze

17. New Sealed Power cam bearings were installed with a special cam bearing tool. The cam bearing bores must be good and clean before installing the new bearings.

18. The cylinder heads received a Valley Head Service Streetmaster porting job. A lot of hand labor goes into a good porting job, plus the experience of knowing just where to remove metal.

19. New cast iron valve guides were pressed in place.

20. Each valve was measured with a micrometer to ensure an exact fit in the corresponding valve guide.

21. The new valve guides were individually honed to fit their matching valve stem.

22. The Crower valve springs were checked on a spring tester for uniformity.

23. The camshaft is a Crower Monarch (No. 09100) hydraulic lifter model which has a duration of 280 degrees.

24. Use assembly lube and plenty of care when inserting the camshaft.

25. Sealed Power bearings were used throughout the engine.

26. Take care when installing the crankshaft so as not to nick or scratch the polished surfaces.

27. Here is one of the Valley Head Service four-bolt main caps being installed. These caps are definitely heavy duty.

28. The caps were torqued in place in steps. Don't attempt to attain the final torque reading all at once.

29. The pistons selected were Speed Pro units (No. 7033P), which are flat top, NHRA, Super Stock-style forged pistons. The listed compression ratio is 10.5:1, but our actual ratio was more like 9.5:1 due to the size of the combustion chamber.

30. Sealed Power rings were used on the Speed Pro pistons.

plugs were installed to wrap up the work on the block. The block was mounted on an engine stand to await final assembly.

The next area of concern was the cylinder heads. Valley Head Service is world famous for their cylinder head work. Many famous racing teams from all types of competition have selected Valley Head Service for their cylinder head needs. Our cylinder heads received a Streetmaster porting job and a Marathon valve job. The Streetmaster porting job is a competition-style porting job for street use. Since the intake ports don't get loaded with carbon quickly, most of the porting work is centered around the exhaust ports. All porting work is done to exacting standards.

The Marathon valve job is a precision three-angle valve job. All the valves are hand-lapped to ensure a positive seal and verify proper valve location. The stock rocker arms were worn, so they were replaced with Sealed Power R-826 replacement units. The stock springs were discarded in favor of new Crower springs. All spring heights were checked, and shims were used to make all installed heights within plus/minus .005-inch. The springs were also checked for any possible binding. Our engine's stock valve guides were sloppy, so they were bored out and replaced with pressed-in 11/32-inch iron guides. The guides were reamed .0005 undersize and hone-fitted to each valve stem. The heads were cc'd and milled to 65cc.

Engine assembly is mostly a matter of replacing all the parts and taking care to check and measure all new pieces. Fitting each individual part is the difference between blueprinting and just rebuilding an engine.

The right camshaft is an important consideration when building a fun engine. We chose a Crower Monarch (No. 09100) hydraulic camshaft and kit. The specs on the camshaft are as follows: duration, 280 degrees; lift, .460 inches. The rpm power range is between 2200 and 6500. The camshaft was coated with Crower assembly lube before being carefully inserted into the block.

The Sealed Power main bearings (No. MS 909P) were installed and lubed prior to setting the crankshaft in place. The Valley Head Service four-bolt main caps were installed and torqued to 65 ft/lbs. The crank was spun to check for freedom of movement, and the end play was checked. An end-play measurement between .002-inch and .007-inch is acceptable; ours was .005-inch. A Sealed Power timing chain (No. 222-489), crank gear (No. 223-262A), and cam gear (No. 223-361) were installed.

The Sealed Power rings were individually measured for end gap and ground on a Sealed Power MT-135 ring grinder. Each ring was squared in the cylinder bore. Acceptable ring end gaps are .012-.020-inch for top rings, .018-.025-inch for the second compression rings, and .015-.055-inch for the oil rings (ours were .016, .014, and .020, respectively.) The rings were installed on the Speed Pro .030-inch overbore pistons (No. 7033P) using a Sealed Power MT-2 ring tool. The listed piston compression ratio is 10.5:1.

The piston and ring assemblies (with the previously installed rods and wrist pins) were generously coated with oil as were the cylinder bores before slipping them into the block. Valley Head Service puts rubber caps over the rod cap studs to protect the cylinder bores and the crankshaft during the installation process. Some type of ring compressor like the Sealed Power MT-117 ring pliers must be used to compress the rings on the piston so they will fit easily into the cylinder bores. The ring compressor must be placed flat against the top of the block so that there isn't any chance of catching a ring on the top of the bore. It will probably be necessary to tap the piston assembly into the block with either a soft-faced mallet or the handle of a hammer. Go slowly when the rod nears the crank so that you can properly position the rod on the crank. Install the rod caps and bearings (in our case, Sealed Power rod bearings No. CB-663P). The caps should be torqued to 30-35 ft/lbs for 11/32-inch-diameter bolts and 40-45 ft/lbs for ⅜-inch-diameter bolts. An easy way to tell which bolts your engine has is to check the size of the nuts; 11/32-inch bolts have ½-inch nuts, and ⅜-inch bolts have 9/16-inch nuts.

After everything is torqued in place, turn the crank over to be sure that there aren't any snags. Next the camshaft should be degreed. There are several ways to degree a cam, and each camshaft manufacturer lists their favorite method in the directions that accompany the cam. Valley Head Service has a specially-degreed aluminum flywheel indicator.

The next step of the block assembly is to add things like the oil pump and fuel pump. Our oil pump is a Sealed Power heavy-duty pump (No. 224-4146) and pump screen (No. 224-1246). The stock oil pan was replaced using the oil pan gasket from a Rocket R-1400 overhaul gasket set. The pan is held in place with Rocket R-960 cad-plated bolts which feature special Sure-Lock washers to prevent loose bolts. The fuel pump is also a Rocket item (No. R-2030). Besides being a high-performance fuel pump, the Rocket pump has the added advantage of being chrome plated. Some nice chrome won't make your engine go any faster, but it is worth plenty of eye-appeal points. We also added some chrome to the front of the engine in the form of a Rocket chromed timing cover (No. R-1094).

Before the cylinder heads were installed, we added another extra-insurance item, a Valley Head Service cylin-

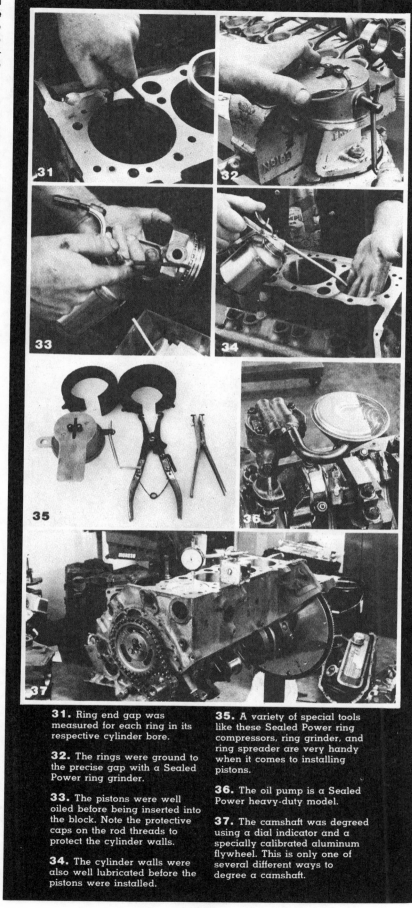

31. Ring end gap was measured for each ring in its respective cylinder bore.

32. The rings were ground to the precise gap with a Sealed Power ring grinder.

33. The pistons were well oiled before being inserted into the block. Note the protective caps on the rod threads to protect the cylinder walls.

34. The cylinder walls were also well lubricated before the pistons were installed.

35. A variety of special tools like these Sealed Power ring compressors, ring grinder, and ring spreader are very handy when it comes to installing pistons.

36. The oil pump is a Sealed Power heavy-duty model.

37. The camshaft was degreed using a dial indicator and a specially calibrated aluminum flywheel. This is only one of several different ways to degree a camshaft.

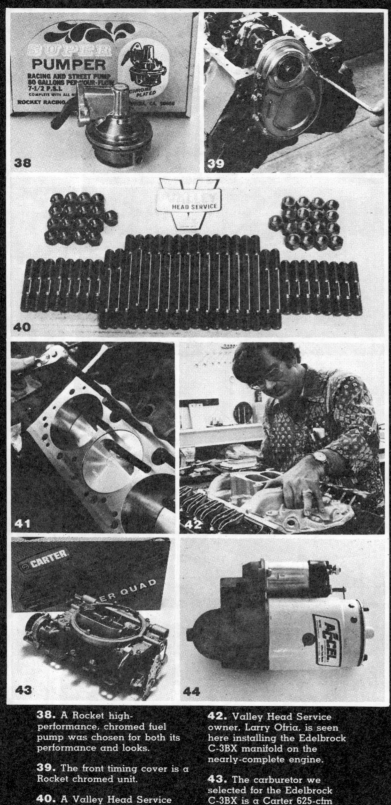

38. A Rocket high-performance, chromed fuel pump was chosen for both its performance and looks.

39. The front timing cover is a Rocket chromed unit.

40. A Valley Head Service cylinder head stud kit was installed to prevent the possibility of stripped head bolts and ease cylinder head installation and removal.

41. The Valley Head Service stud kit is simple to install.

42. Valley Head Service owner, Larry Ofria, is seen here installing the Edelbrock C-3BX manifold on the nearly-complete engine.

43. The carburetor we selected for the Edelbrock C-3BX is a Carter 625-cfm Super Quad with an electric choke.

44. The starter is an Accel Ultra-Tork model which can handle even the toughest starting problems.

der head stud kit. If you've ever struggled to install a heavy cylinder head and line up the head bolts, you'll appreciate the ease of installing heads on studs. The studs also eliminate the all-to-common problem of stripped head bolts. With the Valley Head Service stud kit in place, the Rocket head gaskets were positioned and the cylinder heads installed. The pushrods were slipped into their bores and the rocker arms were tightened.

The intake manifold selected for our fun engine was an Edelbrock C-3BX aluminum unit. The Edelbrock C-3BX manifold was selected because it is especially designed to work on Chevy small-block engines operating in the 1500 to 5500-rpm range, which is right where our engine should run most of the time. Larry Ofria, owner of Valley Head Service, has had very good results with the C-3BX, so he heartily recommended it. The carburetor best matched to the manifold is the Carter No. 9625, which is a 625-cfm, electric-choke, 4-barrel carb. The air cleaner is a Rocket low-restriction 13½-inch-diameter unit (No. R-9483).

To make sure our engine would turn over even on the coldest mornings, we installed an Accel Ultra-Tork starter. The rest of the electrical system is also comprised of Accel parts: Accel spark plugs, Accel silicone spark plug wires, Accel Super Coil, and an Accel dual-point distributor.

Before the Accel distributor was installed, Valley Head Service performed a vital operation—pre-lubing the engine. Valley Head Service markets their own oil pre-lube system, which is inserted through the manifold distributor hole and operated with an electric drill. The Valley Head Service pre-lube system lubes both the upper and lower oil passages to protect against rocker galling and collapsed lifters. It is a good idea to prime the engine before installing the distributor and again prior to firing the engine.

The final additions to our fun engine included a set of Doug Thorley headers (No. 11), designed especially for '55-'57 Chevys. More Rocket dress-up items were added including chromed, ribbed valve covers (No. R-4401), Rocket wire looms, and valve cover wing nuts. The engine was painted bright red, and the combination of the red block and heads, yellow Accel parts, and chrome Rocket goodies makes for an engine that looks as good as it runs.

The proof of our engine came when Larry Ofria hooked it up to Valley Head Service's engine dyno. The engine roared to life on the very first spin of the starter. The sound of an idling, unmuffled 350 will bring a smile to the face of any enthusiast. Larry checked the timing and carburetor adjustments and then ran the engine through its break-in cycle.

The engine sounded great during the

break-in, never missing a beat, but the acid test was still to come. It is always a little tough to see a fresh engine subjected to the rigors of a dyno. It is like driving up against a solid brick wall and trying to push the car through to the other side. As the engine is backed off briefly before trying the next rpm plateau, there is a little relief, but as the engine strains to reach the next level you cringe, half-expecting to see flying parts. We are happy to report that our fun engine came through the dyno trials without a scratch. In fact, the results were very pleasing. The horsepower readings were taken between 2200 and 6000 rpm, with results ranging from 140 horsepower at 2200 rpm to a peak output of 331 horsepower at 5000 rpm. At 5500 rpm, power dropped to 318 horsepower, and at 6000 rpm it fell off further to 310 horsepower. The torque readings were very strong at the lower rpm ranges, gradually tapering off in the higher ranges. This characteristic is just what we wanted, though, because the engine has a great "seat of the pants" kick—you can have the fun of a performance engine without obtaining dragstrip speeds or rpm levels.

At press time the engine had not yet been installed in a vehicle, so on-the-road impressions have to be taken from similar engines that Valley Head Service has built. It has been Larry Ofria's experience that an engine like ours is a near-perfect enthusiast's street powerplant for a variety of vehicles. The power is more than ample for today's driving conditions, the engine is easy to maintain, parts are readily available, and mileage figures are comparable or better than most full-size new cars. A well-built fun engine is the best of all worlds for your Chevy—the ideal combination.

DYNO RESULTS

RPM	HP	TORQUE (ft/lbs)
2200	140	322
2500	164	330
3000	215	360
3500	252	363
4000	298	360
4500	319	344
5000	331	292
5500	318	276
6000	310	225

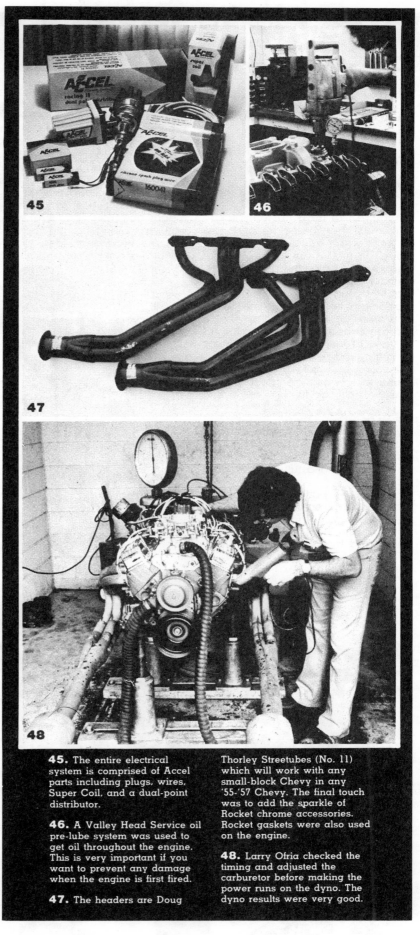

45. The entire electrical system is comprised of Accel parts including plugs, wires, Super Coil, and a dual-point distributor.

46. A Valley Head Service oil pre-lube system was used to get oil throughout the engine. This is very important if you want to prevent any damage when the engine is first fired.

47. The headers are Doug Thorley Streetubes (No. 11) which will work with any small-block Chevy in any '55-'57 Chevy. The final touch was to add the sparkle of Rocket chrome accessories. Rocket gaskets were also used on the engine.

48. Larry Ofria checked the timing and adjusted the carburetor before making the power runs on the dyno. The dyno results were very good.

350 THUNDER

Build An Impressive Chevy Street Motor From The Ground Up

If you're like most custom pickup owners, then there are probably times when you wish your truck would do more than fall on its face when you tromp on the gas. That's especially a problem if you own a late-model smogger, or any year pickup that is propelled with an in-line six. But what can you do? Building an engine is a rather costly proposition, and it's not one of the easiest jobs to tackle for a first-timer, either.

The answer is to take your time, do your research, and then decide if you really want to go through the hassle to upgrade your performance. Many power boosts can be attained by simply going the bolt-on route with the proper carb, intake manifold, headers, and cam. But if you still want to go through with a full buildup, then read on.

Here, we'll be offering some tips on the basics involved in building a Chevy 350 motor from the ground up. This particular engine is a popular one, indeed, and is found in many Chevy pickups. In fact, the 350 is also a pretty popular motor for engine swaps as well, so the venerable beast can also be found in more than a few vintage pickups, too. While the project is being performed on the Chevy 350, first-time builders can refer to this article to see just what is involved in a basic rebuild and buildup project for any engine. The presentation is by no means complete (and that's exactly why we're billing it as the "basics"), so it would be a good idea to have a motor manual or two on hand if you

duplicate our efforts. You will need torque specifications, and a good manual will fill in all the gaps and answer the many and varied questions you will likely come up with during your project.

The first task is to come up with an engine to build. If your truck already has a 350 that's in need of a rebuild, and you don't need it for everyday transportation, then you're in luck. You won't have to shell out the bucks for a second engine to build. If, however, you don't have an engine that can be readily built, then you will have to locate a good 350 to build. You can buy one right in the crate from Chevrolet, but that would be a waste of good cash. There are plenty of good used 350 engines around, and it shouldn't be hard to find one for the right price.

Once the engine is in your hands, it's time to disassemble it and check for potential problems. The heads should be thoroughly checked, as well as the rods and the block itself. Once the disassembly is completed, the block and heads should be sent out to be hot tanked to remove the buildup of grease and grime that has no doubt accumulated over the years. The heads should receive a fresh valve job, and the block should be checked for proper bore. A .030-inch bore job is pretty common unless the cylinders are really in bad shape. Also, the crankshaft usually needs to be reground (ours was ground .010 under), and the block may have to be align bored if the bore of the main crank bearings is off. The connecting rods should be magnafluxed to ensure there are no hairline cracks, then the rods can be reconditioned and balanced if you desire. Having all reciprocating parts balanced is an option that you might also consider. Finally, new cam bearings and freeze plugs are installed, and you are ready to begin assembling your motor.

Our assembly is being handled by Rick Miller of R&J Automotive (501 N. Vineyard Avenue, Ontario, CA 91762). Rick is a hot rodder at heart, and has built more than his share of street and race engines over the years. Since he is very familiar with what it takes to assemble an impressive, yet totally dependable, street motor for everyday use, we left it up to him to come up with the parts lists for this particular motor project.

You can retain many stock parts during the reassembly, but you'd be missing the bet if you didn't go with some of the fine aftermarket high-performance parts that are available. For instance, our project motor received Crane's Thriftmaster Plus camshaft for better fuel economy and great low-to-midrange torque, as well as a Crane steel timing gear and chain for durability. We're also adding an Edelbrock Streetmaster intake manifold and a Carter Thermoquad carb to make the engine perform, and a set of Hooker headers to allow the motor to breathe easier. Mallory's Unilite distributor, electronic ignition coil, and 8mm silicone wires will lend the required fire. And, since we're assembling an "all-new" engine, we're going with 10½-to-1 forged pistons from JE Engineering Corporation to complete the high-performance package. Check out the aftermarket components available, and discuss your needs with a few knowledgeable speed shop hot rodders to come up with a parts list that is right for you.

With the engine secured on an en-

1. Begin by loosening and removing all the bolts and nuts that hold the engine together. It's best to place these in labeled containers to make reassembly easier later.

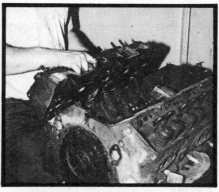

2. Break the engine down completely by removing the intake and carb, heads, pistons, camshaft, and so on. The block will need to be hot tanked to remove the buildup of grime.

3. If you've pulled your engine from a pickup that has been recently running, it shouldn't look like this. This junkyard motor needs lots of work, including all new pistons.

4. Our list of aftermarket parts was carefully chosen by the engine builder, Rick Miller. Be sure that you choose components that will work in harmony for best results.

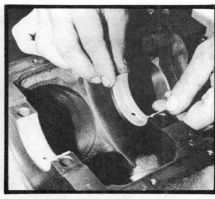

5. Once the machine shop work is completed, the block is secured to an engine stand. First on the agenda is installing new main bearings in the block and in the main caps.

6. Spread special break-in lubricant over all bearing surfaces as shown—and use plenty of it. This will ensure that lubrication is present when the engine is first fired up.

7. The stock crankshaft was retained and bored .010 undersize at the machine shop; main and rod bearings match accordingly. Now set the crankshaft gently in place in the block.

Photography: Steve Stater & Ron Cogan

350 THUNDER

gine stand, you can begin the assembly stage of the project. Install the new main bearings and lubricate them, install the seals, then carefully set the crankshaft in place. The main caps are now installed and torqued to specs. The crank should be spun to ensure freedom of movement, and then crank end play should be checked. Next comes the new Crane camshaft, which is gently slid into place in the block.

The pistons are outfitted with rings, rods, and wrist pins, and then the pistons are slipped into the cylinders with the aid of a ring compressing tool. Each rod receives new rod bearings and is then secured to the crank with

8. The balance of the main bearing caps are now installed. Rick lubricates the bolts for easy threading first, and then torques all main cap bolts to the proper specs.

9. Next, the Crane Thriftmaster Plus camshaft is carefully inserted into the block. New cam bearings were installed at the machine shop when all the machine work was being handled.

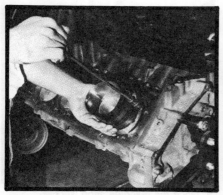

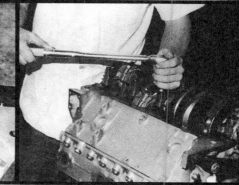

10. After lubricating the piston and ring assembly, and the wrist pins and rods, all are installed in the block as shown. A piston ring compressor must be used for this.

11. Position each rod against the crankshaft as you proceed, and install the bearings and rod caps. These bolts must

also be torqued down to the correct specs.

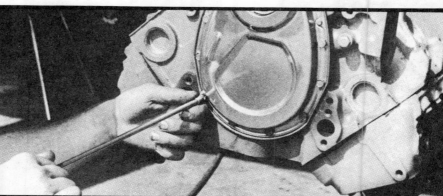

12. The stock timing chain and gear are being discarded in favor of a more durable Crane steel timing gear and chain. A "Chromatized" Rocket timing chain cover is installed next.

the rod caps and torqued down. Following this, the timing chain, timing gear, and cover are installed, and the lifters are oiled and placed in the engine block.

Now it's time to attack the heads. The head gaskets are set in place, and the heads themselves are bolted up to the block. These must also be torqued to specs. Slip the pushrods in the heads, and then bolt up the rocker arms. The rocker arms are tightened down, but not torqued; these will have to be readjusted later. Next follows the installation of the Edelbrock intake manifold, Carter carb, Mallory distributor, and Hooker headers—and the engine work is basically complete.

To add a flashy touch on the 350 engine, we're adding a set of Rocket's latest "Chromatized" accessories such as valve covers, air cleaner, timing chain cover, and thermostat housing. These items are coated by a special process and offer brilliant red, gold, or blue metal tones; we chose

13. The old, worn lifters were chucked out also, and replaced with new lifters from Crane. Rick is shown oiling each lifter before it is slipped into the block.

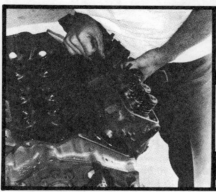
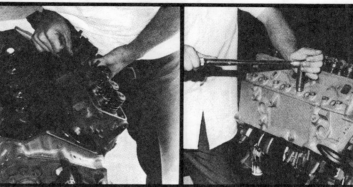

14. The stock heads were sent out to be milled, then received a valve job and Crane valve springs. The head gaskets and heads are now bolted up to the block and torqued down.

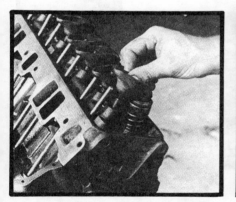

15. Now that the heads are in place, the new pushrods are slipped in the heads, followed by the rocker arms. The rocker arms do not need to be torqued to specific ft.-lbs.

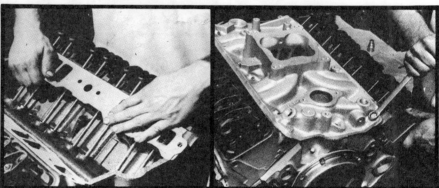

16. The intake comes next. The new manifold gaskets are coated in silicone sealer and then placed on the heads, then the Edelbrock Streetmaster intake manifold is bolted in place.

17. Make sure the number one piston is at top dead center, and then install the distributor and align it for initial timing. We're using a Mallory Unilite distributor here.

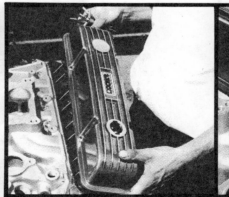

18. To lend a bit of flash on the engine, we're adding the latest hot accessory on the market—Rocket's "Chromatized" valve covers. Ours are gold, but other colors are available.

350 THUNDER

gold for this 350 to accent the color sprayed on the block and heads. Once they are in place, you'll have to install a variety of items like a fuel pump, starter, and so on—and then the motor is ready to go.

Building an engine from the ground up is not the easiest task in the world, but it will result in a motor that you can not only depend on, but one that will offer as much performance as you care to build into it. Since you are the one choosing the parts and doing the actual work, you can build that engine you've always dreamed about. Now, doesn't that get your high-performance taste buds going? We thought so!

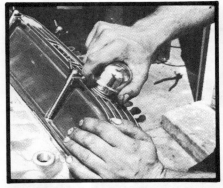

19. The next step is to install the breather on the valve cover as seen here. A PCV valve setup is also being added in the valve cover to satisfy California smog requirements.

20. Now, to add the air/fuel charge to this motor, a Carter 850cfm carburetor is being bolted to the intake manifold. Rejetting will be investigated after the engine is fired up.

21. And what is a nicely built engine without custom header exhaust? You know the answer. So, a set of Hooker headers takes the place of the stock exhaust manifolds.

22. All new engines should receive a brand new thermostat, and ours is no exception. A gold Rocket thermostat housing is being bolted up for a nice touch.

23. Also, to coordinate with the rest of the gold accessories, a Rocket air cleaner is being added. Again, a fitting must be added to the bottom for the PCV hose to be smog-legal.

24. Substantial Mallory 8mm silicone ignition wires are also added to carry the fire. A Mallory electronic ignition coil will be used when the engine is dropped in the truck.

25. Many small items need to be added, such as an oil pan, starter, fuel pump, and so on—but the engine is basically finished. And we can't wait to try it out!

BUILDING A BLOWN CHEVY 350

HOW TO DOUBLE THE HORSEPOWER OF A SMALL-BLOCK CHEVY WITH EASY-TO-INSTALL, BOLT-ON SPEED EQUIPMENT

By Bruce Caldwell

This is the third and final installment of HOT ROD's Budget Engine Buildup series, and just as in drag racing and football, we saved the best for last. This is the Top Fuel final and the Super Bowl all wrapped up in one: the world's best high-performance powerplant, the small-block Chevrolet. A lot of brand loyalty is prevalent with performance enthusiasts, but when you reduce the brand controversy to facts and common sense, the small-block Chevrolet is your best bolt-on high-performance bargain. A large part of the reason for the success of the little Chevy is the engineering behind the engine. It is a very well-designed engine that readily responds to basic performance tuning.

When people get together to bench race about their favorite engines, they like to throw around impressive figures. Big numbers make great conversation but they rarely do

anything for everyday street driveability. Hot rodders who are honest with themselves know that it doesn't take 700 horsepower to make a very enjoyable street motor. Realistically, any motor that puts out over 300 horsepower and good bottom-end torque is a plenty potent street motor. And it is one that you can live with every day, the kind that is dependable and easy to operate and maintain.

When you talk about percentages, our 350 smogger Chevy made some very impressive horsepower gains. The improvement from stock to our final stage resulted in more than a 100-percent increase in horsepower and a 46-percent increase in torque. In terms of horsepower, our simple bolt-on modifications were worth

over 200 ponies—not too shabby considering we started with a dead-stock 1978 350-cubic-inch smog motor, and we went no further into the engine than to change the camshaft. Everything else was bolted to the outside of the engine.

This installment, besides proving the potential of the small-block Chevy, proved that a blower can simply be bolted on and run without modifying the engine. A properly set-up street blower like the Dyer Street Charger that we used is a bolt-on proposition, not some tenuous racing

BUILDING A BLOWN CHEVY 350

equipment loose on the street.

We conducted our tests at the impressive W.R. Grace Dynamometer Test Facility in Garden Grove, California. The test center serves as a research and development department for all Grace high-performance products like Mallory ignitions, Mr. Gasket, Brooks pistons, Blackjack headers, Team G manifolds, Hays clutches and Lakewood chassis products. The man in charge of our project was Art Chrisman, ably assisted by Gene Adams and Mike Chrisman. The engine arrived in a crate from Chevrolet, the same engine you would find in any '78 Chevy equipped with the 350 option. There was absolutely nothing special about this engine. It was a standard late-model production engine. In fact,

earlier versions of the 350 should be expected to perform even better, due to less-restrictive pre-smog parts on most of them.

STEP NO. 1:
STOCK ENGINE

Step No. 1 was to break the engine in and run it just as it came from Chevrolet—dead stock. The engine was the same engine as any customer would receive from Chevrolet if he ordered a factory-fresh motor. The engine was an 8.5:1 compression, unleaded fuel smog motor. The timing was set at the factory specs of 6° @ 650 rpm, which gives a total advance of 28° @ 4000 rpm.

The stock cast-iron manifolds were employed; but to make the dyno hookup easier, dual turbo-style muf-

flers were used with 2½-inch tailpipes. The stock air cleaner was used with an air flow transducer. The air flow transducer is a dyno device that raises the air cleaner about 18 inches to get an air supply that is more representative of normal driving conditions. Peak power achieved in step No. 1 was 186 horsepower at 4000 rpm. The peak torque was 288 ft.-lbs. at 3000 rpm. The peak horsepower produced by a similar engine with the catalytic converter and single factory exhaust would have been even less than the 186 horsepower achieved with the dual exhaust system.

STEP NO. 2:
HEADERS

For ease of modification and low

Our series of dyno tests were conducted on the W.R. Grace Company's research and development dynamometer in Garden Grove, California. Here is the stock 1978 350-cubic-inch small-block Chevy as it was run in stock form. What appears to be an ultra-high-rise air cleaner is actually an air flow transducer, commonly used for dyno tests. Note that the transducer is rigged for test readings. The 350 was a smog engine even down to the smog-type, low-compression pistons.

For Step No. 7, a Holley spread-bore carburetor was installed on the Weiand two-plane manifold. The 650-cfm carb turned out to be better suited for the engine than the larger 850-cfm double-pumper that was installed in Step No. 8. A Mallory Unilite ignition was tried in place of the Chevy HEI system, and little, if any, difference was noticed.

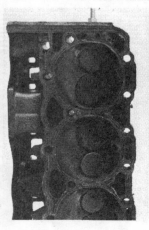

The engine as it appeared in Step No. 7—your basic and very worthwhile hot-rodded engine. For the money invested, an engine in this state provides excellent performance. The Blackjack headers have a special aluminum coating which greatly improves the lifespan of the headers. Besides the stock cylinder heads on the left, a set of Chevy Turbo heads (right) were tried on the engine. The Turbo heads were modified by Cylinder Heads America.

cost, step No. 2 was a real winner. All that was done was to install a set of Blackjack headers and a Mr. Gasket low-restriction air cleaner. The Blackjack headers had 1¾-inch primary tubes that were 32 inches long with 3-inch-diameter collectors. These two simple changes really improved the breathing ability of the small-block, and peak power jumped to 224 horsepower at 4250 rpm. Peak torque was reached at 3000 rpm with a reading of 312 ft.-lbs. Giving the engine a little breathing room was worth almost 40 horsepower, or a 20-percent increase over step No. 1: proof positive that headers are one of the best performance buys.

STEP NO. 3:
MORE ADVANCE

Step No. 3 involved just the use of a timing light and a distributor wrench. The initial timing was advanced 8° to 14° for a total advance of 36°. Both power and torque went up slightly to 231 horsepower at 4250 rpm and 321 ft.-lbs. at 2500 rpm. No new parts were added, but the power was up 45 ponies with just the addition of headers, a dual exhaust system with turbo-style mufflers, and a low-restriction air cleaner, plus the simple act of advancing the timing. A very nice gain for very little expense and effort.

STEP NO. 4:
NEW MANIFOLD

The fourth step involved the installation of an aftermarket aluminum manifold, in this case a Team G Weiand two-plane manifold. An adapter was used to mate the Team G manifold to the stock Quadrajet carburetor. Horsepower went up only 7 units, but the rpm range was extended as peak power occurred at 4500 rpm. Peak torque dropped a little to 314 ft.-lbs. at 3500 rpm.

STEP NO. 5:
CAM CHANGE

Changing cams was the most involved step in this series as far as getting into the engine goes. A cam change is still considered a bolt-on modification, because the change can be made with the engine in the car and without completely disassembling the engine. A cam change is definitely more involved than adding headers.

The cam used was a Chevy factory L-82 Corvette cam, part No. 3896962. All other factors were the same as before, including the timing and the AC part No. R45TS spark plugs. Fuel for all the tests was Daeco high-

octane for consistent dyno results. Fuel pressure was 6½ pounds using the stock fuel pump backed with the dyno's electric fuel pump. Oil pressure was 35 pounds at idle and 48 pounds at 3000 rpm with the engine warmed up. Water temperature was held at 170°.

The cam seemed to work quite well with the Team G manifold, as horsepower increased to a peak of 263 horsepower at 5000 rpm. Again the power range was extended. The peak torque leveled off at 312 ft.-lbs. at 3500 rpm.

STEP NO. 6:
NEW IGNITION

Step No. 6 proved that often the factory equipment is very good. The stock Chevrolet HEI (high energy ignition) system is a well-designed unit that provides excellent spark for any mild street engine. The HEI unit was replaced with a Mallory Unilite infrared ignition. Total timing advance was still 36°, with total spark obtained at 2800 rpm. The new ignition was good for exactly one more horsepower and one more foot-pound of torque than the stock Chevy ignition. The Mallory unit would undoubtedly be a good improvement over earlier engines that came with standard point-type ignitions, but in the case of newer engines with the HEI, it wasn't a great horsepower-per-dollar value.

STEP No. 7:
SPREAD-BORE CARBURETOR

A very typical carburetor change was made for step No. 7: the addition of a 650-cfm Holley spread-bore carburetor. This is a standard Quadrajet replacement carburetor commonly used with aftermarket manifolds. Horsepower increased to 278 at 5000 rpm, and peak torque increased to 322 ft.-lbs. at 3500 rpm.

At the end of step No. 7, the engine was at the stage very often matched by many bolt-on hop-up artists, and the power was up almost 100 horsepower over stock: a nice improvement that was easily obtained. An engine built to this stage won't win any Bracket I trophies, but it is a very responsive and enjoyable street engine, within the reach and budget of most enthusiasts.

STEP No. 8:
TOO MUCH CARBURETION

Steps 8, 9, 10 and 11 were done to

illustrate what can happen when a motor is overbuilt. Very often biggest isn't always best, yet many enthusiasts think they will get gobs of power by simply installing a killer cam or a mega-cfm induction system on a relatively stock engine. These parts need to be used on an engine set up to accept their potential.

For step No. 8, a Holley 850-cfm double-pumper carburetor was substituted for the smaller Holley spread-bore carb used in step No. 7. Peak power stayed the same with 278 horsepower at 5000 rpm, and peak torque improved slightly to 335 ft.-lbs. at 3500 rpm. The whole power curve moved up slightly, but for all practical purposes the change didn't really improve the engine enough to warrant buying a bigger carburetor. In its present state, the engine wasn't able to use the increased capacity of the double-pumper carburetor.

STEP NO. 9:
TOO MUCH CAM

The installation of a big cam in an engine with stock heads and stock valvetrain can be a real waste, as we realized when one of the largest hydraulic cams available was installed. The cam was a Crane CCH-300-NC, which has a lift of 252 degrees and a duration of 300 degrees with a gross valve lift of .521-inch. Crane recommends that this cam be used in an engine with a large-cfm single carb or multiple carburetion, a single-plane manifold or a tunnel-ram, large-tube headers and modified cylinder heads. Crane knows what they are talking about because the cam wasn't made for our 350 in its present state. Power and torque both fell off through the low and medium ranges, and peak power wasn't any better than before the cam was installed. Peak power was 277 horsepower at 5250 rpm, and peak torque was 326 ft.-lbs. at 4000 rpm. Bottom-end horsepower was actually lower than that achieved with the stock engine.

STEP NO. 10:
BIG HEADERS

Crane said that big headers were needed for their CCH-300-NC cam, so the Blackjack street headers were removed and dyno race headers were bolted in place. The dyno headers have 1¾x32-inch primaries and 4-inch collectors. Very low-restriction dyno mufflers were also used. The power picked up to 290 horsepower at 5000 rpm, and peak torque

BUILDING A BLOWN CHEVY 350

jumped to 341 ft.-lbs. at 4000 rpm.

STEP NO. 11:
TRICK CYLINDER HEADS

Another recommendation for the Crane cam was modified cylinder heads, so a set of Cylinder Heads America NASCAR turbo heads were tried on the engine. The CHA heads had smaller combustion chambers, which raised the compression ratio to 9.5-to-1. The power curve was raised across the board, and peak power ended up at 324 horsepower at 5500 rpm. Peak torque was 364 ft.-lbs. at 4000 rpm.

STEP NO. 12:
BACKTRACKING

For step No. 12, the big cam was removed and the factory L-82 cam was reinstalled, as were the Black-jack street headers. The surprising finding was that power was about the same, with peak power actually 2 horsepower greater than in step No. 11. Peak torque was down to 342 ft.-lbs. at 3500 to 4500 rpm. Low- and mid-range torque were also down from that obtained with the big Crane cam.

Step No. 12 was far as we went with the normally aspirated engine. Power was up 140 horsepower, and the usable rpm range was extended from 4000 to 5500 rpm.

STEP NO. 13:
DYER STREET CHARGER

For the last part of the Chevy 350-cubic-inch small-block bolt-on dyno test, we decided to install the ultimate bolt-on performance part, a Dyer Street Charger Roots-style blower. The engine was returned to step No. 7 configuration and the blower was installed. The Dyer kit came complete with everything necessary to bolt on and go. The blower was underdriven 11 percent for street usage and came with two specially prepared 750-cfm Carter carburetors. There is a choke provision so the engine still started easily. The installation was straightforward. Dyer has taken all the guesswork out of installing a blower—it is really just a simple bolt-on operation.

Power and torque reading both took tremendous leaps with the installation of the Dyer Street Charger. The gains were substantial over the stock engine and even the modified engine as tested in step No. 12. Peak power was 382 horsepower at 5500 rpm, and peak torque was 416 ft.-lbs. at 4000 rpm. The spark advance was set at 35° total advance, and the spark plugs were changed to Champion BL57s. Water temperature remained at 170°. The blower boost ranged from 4 pounds at 2200 rpm to 9.5 pounds at 5500 rpm.

STEP NO. 14:
LOOKING FOR 400 HP

Everyone was very pleased with the way the engine performed with the Dyer blower but felt that the engine was capable of putting out more power. In an attempt to gain entrance to the 400-horsepower level, the dyno headers were reinstalled. They boosted horsepower and peak torque slightly to 388 horsepower and 416 ft.-lbs., respectively. Remember these figures were obtained with an engine that was totally untouched internally and had the undesirable smog pistons. It was felt that better pistons would easily have moved the peak power over the 400 mark.

Looking at the results realistically,

The Dyer Street Charger uses a specially machined plate to adapt the blower to an aluminum dual-quad aftermarket manifold. The plate restricts the air flow in keeping with the street usage that the blower is set up for. It would be easy enough to make more horsepower, but Dyer knows through years of experience what really works best on the street.

Dyer's Machine Service (7665 W. 63rd St., Argo, IL 60501) specially modifies a pair of Carter 750-cfm carburetors for use with the Dyer Street Charger blower system. The rear carburetor has a choke, so cold-starting is no problem. Dyer installs strip kits in the Competition Series Carter carbs.

The Dyer Street Charger is completely set up and ready to install as it comes from the crate. Dyer sets all tolerances with street driving in mind. Mike Chrisman and Gene Adams literally bolted the impressive blower to the top of the 350 Chevy and it was ready to run. The Dyer blower kit comes complete with everything needed for the installation.

You're looking at a virtually stock '78 350-cubic-inch Chevrolet smog motor that puts out almost 400 horsepower. The addition of a Dyer Street Charger blower and a few bolt-on speed pieces more than doubled the horsepower of the engine. The looks alone are worth the price of admission for the Dyer blower, but besides the looks and power, the engine is completely streetable. This blown small-block offers the best of all worlds.

the figure of 388 horsepower was very respectable and as much power as most people can ever use on the street anyway. Gary Dyer admitted that it would be easy enough to push the blower much higher, but his many years of preparing blowers for street use lead him to this present combination. The idea with a street blower is to achieve a livable compromise between performance and driveability. The Dyer Street Charger is a well-thought-out unit that provides more than ample power when you want it, good dependable street operation (we know of many cases of Dyer-equipped cars making cross-country treks without incident), and more peer group status than any other single piece of performance equipment.

Looking back over the results obtained by Art Chrisman and Gene Adams on the W.R. Grace dynamometer test facility, three tests stand out: step No. 3, step No. 7 and step No. 13. Depending on your needs and finances, three very nice engines could be built following those three steps. Step No. 3 was a great starting point, easily accomplished for ap-

proximately $100 and a couple of hours. Step No. 7 was a well-balanced bolt-on aftermarket package within the abilities and budget of the average enthusiast. Step No. 13 was the ultimate bolt-on engine modification which showed how easy it is to bolt on over 200 horsepower.

This isn't a new revelation, but we will repeat it anyway: The small-block Chevrolet engine is an extremely well-engineered engine that responds readily to performance modifications. It is the best value in all of hot rodding, a distinction the small-block Chevy has held for 25 years. **HR**

HORSEPOWER TEST PHASE

ENGINE SPEED	1	2	3	4	5	6	7	8	9	10	11	12	13	14
2000	100.4	107.6	113.9	112	103.2	101.4	103.7	108.9	82.1	82.4	102.2	100.9		
2200													144	151.2
2500	136	146.4	153	148	134.3	132	142.8	146.6	138.3	138.7	155.2	147.1	174.9	180.9
3000	164.7	178.8	182	177.7	176.9	175.8	180.9	188.5	184.8	193.2	203.6	192.3	226.9	231.1
3500	185.1	205	212.4	209.3	208.3	208.9	214.8	223.5	212	225.5	241.2	228.1	272	276.9
4000	186.5	223.7	230.5	233	237.9	236.8	243.3	253.4	248.5	259.8	277.7	260.6	316.9	322.7
4250	184.9	224.2	230.9											
4500	179	218.4	230.2	238.3	255.9	256.9	266.6	273.3	272.7	285.1	302.9	293.5	354.2	360.7
4750			225.3	231.4										
5000					263.3	264.5	277.7	277.5	276.7	290.4	313.2	315.6	375.6	380
5250					259				276.7	285.4		322.7	378.2	388
5500										285	324.4	326.5	382	
5750										274				
6000											316.3			

TORQUE TEST PHASE

ENGINE SPEED	1	2	3	4	5	6	7	8	9	10	11	12	13	14
2000	263.6	282.4	299	294.1	270.8	266.1	272.4	285.8	215.7	216.3	251.4	264.9		
2200													345.7	360.7
2500	285.6	296.8	321.2	310.8	281.9	277.2	300.2	307.8	290.2	291	301.2	308.9	367.4	379.8
3000	288.3	312.9	318.4	311.1	309	297.1	316.9	329.8	323.4	338.1	356.2	336.5	391.6	404.4
3500	277.6	296.7	318.4	313.8	312.3	313.2	322.3	335.3	317.8	338.1	361.7	342.1	407.4	415.4
4000	244.8	293.5	301.8	305.7	312.3	310.8	319.6	332.5	326.1	340.9	364.5	342.1	416	423.5
4250	228.3	276.7	285.2											
4500	208.9	254.8	268.6	278	298.5	299.7	311.3	318.8	318.1	332.6	353.5	342.4	413.2	420.8
4750			249.2	255.7										
5000					276.4	277.7	291.9	291.3	290.5	305	328.9	331.4	394.3	399
5250					259.8				276.9	285		323	378.2	688
5500										272	309.7	312	365	
5750										250				
6000											276.8			

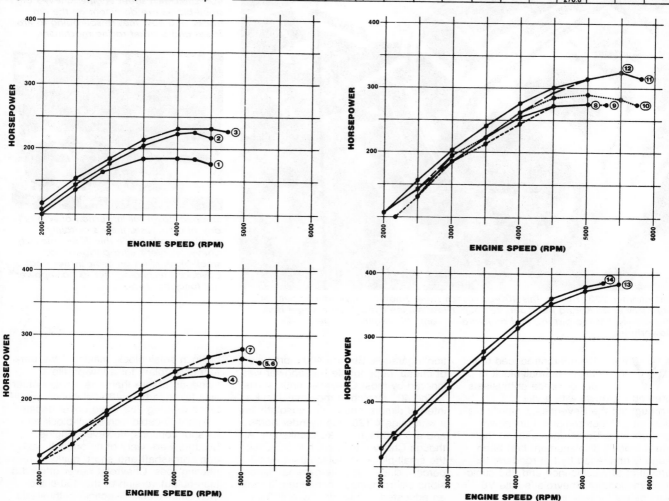

SECRET WEAPON

WITH 400 CUBIC INCHES AND 500 HORSEPOWER, THIS STREET SMALL-BLOCK IS FULL OF SURPRISES

Scooter Brothers applied his oval track racing expertise to developing a 400-cubic-inch street engine. Chevy's big small-blocks are dominant on the dirt tracks, and now they're spreading to Pro Street and bracket racing machinery.

Stripped down for inspection after a full day of dyno tests, there's certainly nothing exotic inside this 400-cubic-inch Chevy. Scooter's ultra-performance small-block relies on cubic inches and advanced technology for its horsepower, not fancy hardware.

Just another 283? Hardly. This 400-cubic-inch street small-block produced over 500 horsepower on Racing Head Service's SuperFlow engine dyno. With a single Holley four-barrel, flat-top pistons, and an hydraulic cam, this engine is a low-profile powerhouse.

When Chevrolet introduced the 400-cubic-inch small-block in 1970, performance enthusiasts greeted its arrival with a yawn. Throughout the Seventies, Chevy's biggest small-block remained unknown and unloved. Earlier increases in the small-block's displacement had been eagerly embraced by hot rodders; the arrival of 327-cubic-inch and 350-cubic-inch versions of Chevrolet's little V8 was cause for celebration in the na-

tion's garages. But the 400's promise of cheap, dependable horsepower was ignored by most Chevrolet enthusiasts.

The 400 stretched the small-block's internal dimensions to the absolute limit with huge 4.125-inch cylinder bores and a 3.750-inch-stroke crankshaft. Although Chevy engineers had increased the small-block's displacement by 50 percent since 1955, its external dimensions still remained unchanged. It took an educated eye to identify a 400-cu-

bic-inch small-block, making it the perfect powerplant for a low-profile "sleeper." More than one unwary racer was taken in by a 400-cubic-inch small-block wearing 283 valve cover decals.

The 400-cubic-inch small-block had its shortcomings, however. Engine builders were wary of its oddball cast iron crankshaft and short, quirky connecting rods. Chevrolet never offered a high-output version of the 400-cubic-inch small-block. Skeptical enthusiasts

Third freeze plug in center of block identifies this early 400-cubic-inch casting. This plug was eliminated in later castings, but the raised pad remained.

Scooter selected a used block with four-bolt main bearing caps for his 400-cubic-inch small-block experiments. 400 blocks have larger main bearing bores than other small-blocks; bolt holes for bearing caps are moved outward.

400 blocks have siamesed cylinder walls and huge 4.125-inch cylinder bores. Coolant does not circulate between adjacent cylinders; holes in deck surface prevent formation of steam pockets in water jacket. 400-cubic-inch small-blocks are susceptible to head gasket problems because there is little support for gasket between cylinders.

Counterweight on flywheel flange helps balance 400 crankshaft.

Painted lifter valley makes block cleaning easy. Sealed surface helps oil return to pan quickly.

dismissed the oversize mouse motor as an engine suited to station wagons and four-door Biscaynes. The headline in one performance magazine characterized Chevy's new creation as "The 400-inch Bust." In this environment, the 400-cubic-inch small-block seemed to be an engine without a future in high-performance. After all, if an engine builder needed cubic inches, Chevrolet's big-block V8s were an inexhaustible source of horsepower.

It took 10 years for the 400-cubic-inch small-block to come out of the shadows. Credit the nation's oval track racers with discovering the 400's performance potential in the early Eighties. Dirt trackers found that the 400 offered tremendous torque in a lightweight, compact package. Today, the 400-cubic-inch small-block is virtually standard equipment for sprint cars and unlimited late-model stock cars. Now another group has noticed the 400's features:

Chevy's biggest small-block is the new favorite of serious street performance enthusiasts.

Scooter Brothers has seen the 400-cubic-inch small-block soar in popularity. As one of the partners in Racing Head Service's huge engine building enterprise in Memphis, Tennessee, Scooter saw Chevy's biggest small-block establish its dominance on the dirt tracks. Now Scooter has undertaken a program to make the 400-cubic-inch Chevy the undisputed king of the boulevards as well. Under the watchful eye of the shop's computerized Super-Flow dyno, Scooter and the RHS crew have developed a legitimate *500*-horsepower street small-block.

Scooter's small-block reached this lofty power level without the aid of any "unnatural" accessories. There are no blowers or nitrous injectors to be seen—just a box-stock Holley four-barrel and a hot hydraulic cam. The "secret" behind this small-block's awesome dyno numbers is advanced technology. Scooter is the walking definition of a car enthusiast; he probably bleeds 40-weight racing oil when he skins his knuckles, and wakes up at

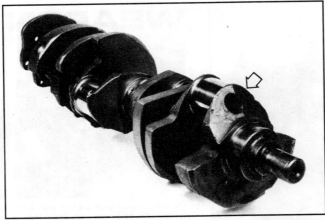

Nodular cast iron 400-cubic-inch small-block crank has 3.750-inch stroke and oversize 2.650-inch main bearing journals. Note stock lightening hole in first rod throw.

Externally balanced 400-cubic-inch small-blocks must use special harmonic dampeners and flexplates. Counterweights (arrows) offset 400's long stroke.

Crankshaft journals are reground, indexed, and micropolished. Note chamfered oil holes.

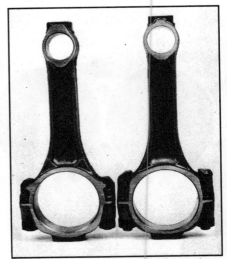

Stock 400 connecting rod (left) has short rod bolts, 5.565-inch center-to-center length. Scooter installs 5.700-inch-long 350-type rods with high-strength fasteners in his high-performance 400s.

night reciting cylinder head casting numbers. Coming up with an ultra-performance Chevrolet was a challenge Scooter couldn't resist.

THE SCIENCE OF STREET PERFORMANCE

The small-block Chevrolet V8 is the foundation of the entire speed equipment industry. Ever since the small-block dethroned the flathead as America's favorite performance engine, Chevy's little V8 has been the object of intense scrutiny. From high-rise manifolds to deep-sump oil pans, the small-block Chevrolet accounts for the majority of speed equipment sales. But with a few exceptions, the development of street performance small-blocks has largely been a haphazard process—until now.

Scooter adopted a scientific approach to street performance when he set out to develop a super small-block for RHS' line of mail-order engines. Racers rely on engine dynos and lap times to gauge their progress, but most street enthusiasts depend on the seat of their pants to monitor their efforts.

The street performance scene is changing rapidly, however. The distinctions between street cars and race cars are becoming blurred; the burgeoning "Pro Street" movement mimics the performance as well as the appearance of race track machinery. Engine building techniques that once were reserved for all-out racing engines are being applied to serious street motors. With computer designed cam profiles, flow-tested cylinder heads, and development time on automated dynamometers, today's street performance small-block has the credentials of a purebred competition engine.

Scooter recognized that his maximum-effort street machine engine would have to cope with traffic jams and service station gasoline. He planned to take full advantage of the 400-cubic-inch small-block's large displacement. The extra inches of Chevrolet's biggest small-block would allow him to assemble a relatively mild engine combination. Instead of relying on a radical cam profile, multiple carburetion, and an extreme compression ratio, Scooter's streetworthy small-block

owes its performance to its displacement. As one sage of hot rodding once observed, "There's no substitute for cubic inches . . ."

BIG-BORE BLOCKS

Scooter selected a well-seasoned 400 block for his street engine development program. There are several ways to spot a 400 block among the hundreds of cores lined up in RHS' storeroom. First, Scooter looks for *three* freeze plugs in both sides of the block. In later castings, the middle plug is deleted, but a raised pad in place of the "missing" third freeze plug identifies a 400 block. A casting number that ends with the numerals "509" also denotes a big-bore small-block. Scooter searched until he found a core with four-bolt main bearing caps.

The 400 is a maverick. It is the only small-block with 2.650-inch-diameter

RHS replaces stock cast aluminum dished piston with flat-top Venolia forging. Valve reliefs in custom-made Venolia piston match intake and exhaust valve diameters.

Aftermarket steel flywheel is drilled for proper balance with 400 crankshaft.

Scooter selected early-Seventies cylinder heads with large combustion chambers for his ultra-performance 400-cubic-inch small-block. Holes drilled in deck surface match steam holes in block.

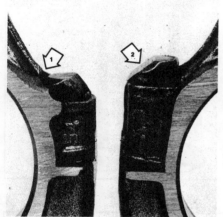

Shoulder of 400 connecting rod (1) is deeply notched for bolt head; this relief weakens the rod at a critical area. Rod bolt head (2) must be chamfered for cam clearance when 350 rod is used with long-stroke 400 crank.

main bearing journals; other small-blocks built since late 1968 have 2.450-inch main bearings. The 400's 4.125-inch-diameter bores are so large that the walls of adjacent cylinders are joined; no water circulates between these "siamesed" cylinders. Despite these important internal changes, the 400-cubic-inch Chevy retains all of the small-block V8's familiar external dimensions. The 400 enjoys virtually unlimited parts interchangeability with other small-blocks. Cylinder heads, manifolds, cams, valvetrain components, and oiling systems can be swapped freely.

After a thorough visual inspection for flaws and stripped bolt holes, Scooter's used 400 block was carefully tested for cracks with Magnaflux dry magnetic powder. The RHS machinists pay special attention to the main bearing webs and the outer water jacket when examining a block. The block is then milled

to ensure that its deck surfaces are straight and parallel to the crankshaft centerline. The cylinders are bored oversize and then honed to 4.155-inch diameter. Torque plates bolted to the block during the honing operation recreate the stresses which occur when the head bolts are tightened during final assembly. This honing technique improves the quality of the piston ring seal. After the block is thoroughly cleaned, its lifter valley is painted to seal the pores of the metal. The painted valley also speeds the flow of oil back to the pan.

All 400-cubic-inch small-blocks have 3.750-inch-stroke nodular cast iron crankshafts. Scooter has found that these stock cranks are perfectly satisfactory for high-performance street engines. The large diameter of the main bearing journals certainly contributes to the crankshaft's surprising strength. Crank preparation is straightforward at RHS: the core is Magnaflux inspected, then the rod and main journals are reground, indexed, and micropolished.

The 400-cubic-inch Chevy is the only externally balanced small-block: The crankshaft counterweights are not large enough to offset the 400's extremely long stroke, so Chevrolet engineers added extra counterweights to the har-

monic balancer and flywheel (or flexplate when the engine is used with an automatic transmission). A 400-cubic-inch small-block *must* have the correct balancer and flywheel—unless the crankshaft has been internally balanced by installing slugs of heavy metal in the counterweights. This is an expensive procedure that is difficult to justify for a street engine. RHS electronically balanced the crank for Scooter's test engine with a standard 400 counterweighted dampener and flywheel.

LONG RODS FOR THE 400

One weakness of the 400 small-block is its connecting rods. The 400 rods are .135-inch shorter than other small-block rods (5.565-inch center-to-center length vs. 5.700-inch), and they use shorter through-bolts. These connecting rod revisions make sense for a low-performance engine. Shortening the rods' center-to-center distance leaves more room for the rings on a stock piston, and shortening the rod bolts prevents interference with the cam lobes. Unfortunately, these changes have some undesirable side effects. The combination of a short rod length and a long stroke produces a rod-to-stroke ratio of only 1.48:1. The angle

Sharp edges in intake valve bowl are carefully blended; three-angle valve seats improve airflow. Large 76cc combustion chamber yields 10:1 compression ratio with flat-top pistons.

Intake runners are matched to manifold; grinding extends only ¾-inch into port. Rough finish in port aids fuel atomization.

Exhaust port is the bottleneck in stock Chevy heads. RHS enlarges and polishes the exhaust runner to remove this restriction.

Venolia piston has shorter compression height than stock 400 cast piston to compensate for longer 350 connecting rod. Ring grooves are machined for ⁵⁄₆₄-inch-wide compression rings.

Stainless steel 2.02-inch-diameter intake valves and 1.600-inch exhausts regulate airflow through Scooter's street small-block.

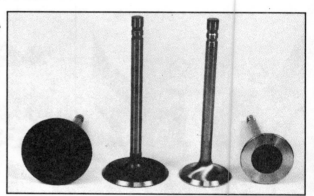

formed by the rod and crank throw is quite severe, which increases the stress on the piston skirts and cylinder walls. (For comparison, rod-to-stroke ratios for other small-blocks range from 1.9:1 in a 302-cubic-inch small-block to 1.63:1 for a 350-cubic-inch Chevy.) In addition, the factory machines deep notches in the shoulders of all 400 small-block connecting rods to accommodate the short bolts. These bolt head reliefs weaken the rod forks at a critical point.

Scooter's solution is to use rods from a 350-cubic-inch small-block. He believes that the 350-type rod is more reliable in a high-performance application, and points out that its longer center-to-center dimension improves the rod angularity. The longer 350 rods also lower the loads on the piston skirts and extend engine life.

RHS uses selected 350 rod cores which are inspected, shotpeened, and resized. The only modification required to install the 350 rods in a 400-cubic-inch small-block is to slightly bevel several bolt heads for camshaft clearance. The amount of metal removed is slight, and does not noticeably weaken the bolt. The 400 and 350 rods both have 2.225-inch-diameter big end bores and use the same bearing inserts. The RHS

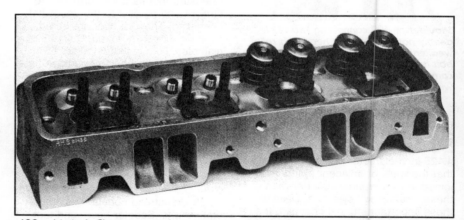

400-cubic-inch Chevy responds to airflow improvement offered by Brodix -10 aluminum heads. High-compression Brodix heads added over 50 horsepower and raised peak power from 5500 to 6500 rpm.

crew assembled Scooter's engine with standard Clevite high-performance bearings.

Stock 400-cubic-inch small-block pistons cannot be used with 5.700-inch-long 350 connecting rods because their compression height is too long. Fortunately, there are several piston options for a long-rod 400-cubic-inch small-block. Speed Pro offers a flat-top forged piston with two valve reliefs for this combination (part No. 7066P). This

piston is only available for a 4.155-inch bore size, and it is machined for ⁵⁄₆₄-inch-wide piston rings. Scooter used these pistons in his development motor, but he later switched to custom-made Venolia pistons. The Venolias can be ordered with virtually any bore size and ring groove combination. This gives an engine builder more flexibility in his choice of components. Scooter recommends .004-inch skirt-to-wall clearance for these pistons.

WEAPON

RHS head porters enlarged Brodix -10 intake runners to 200cc. These heads are often used on oval track racing engines.

Brodix heads' small 64cc combustion chambers raised compression to 11.6:1 on Scooter's super small-block. Hardened inserts provide long valve seat life.

Competition Cams roller rockers pivot on stock-type rocker balls. Grooves supply lubrication to prevent galling.

RHS machined Chevy heads for screw-in rocker arm studs. Stock pressed studs can pull out at high rpm.

Magnum valve springs are installed at 100 pounds seat pressure. Stock steel retainers, umbrella oil shields, and stamped split locks are used.

Stock Edelbrock Victor Jr. intake manifold was used throughout dyno tests. Holley 4779 750cfm double-pumper carburetor retained stock jetting.

Valvetrain includes Competition Cams Magnum roller-tip rocker arms with 1.52:1 ratio.

CYLINDER HEAD EXPERIMENTS

Airflow is crucial to an engine's performance on the street and on the race track. There is certainly no lack of cylinder head expertise at Racing Head Service. Scooter's men in the grinding room prepared a set of early-Seventies heads (casting No. 441) for his development engine. These heads have the same generous runners as the famous "fuel-injection" heads of the Sixties, but they also have large 76cc combustion chambers. Big combustion chambers are essential for a street 400 because they keep the compression ratio within reason. Even with flat-top pistons, the compression ratio in Scooter's test engine worked out to 10:1, thanks to the enormous swept volume of the 400-cubic-inch small-block's cylinders.

Scooter knew that the stock exhaust ports in cast iron heads were very restrictive. The exhaust runners were fully ported and polished to eliminate this bottleneck. The intake runners were untouched except for minor blending in the valve bowls. Flow bench tests have convinced Scooter that the valve seats should be as high as possible in the combustion chambers. The three-angle valve job consists of a narrow 15-degree top cut, a 45-degree seat (.100-inch wide), and a 60-degree bottom

cut. Scooter selected 2.02-inch-diameter stainless steel intake valves and 1.600-inch stainless exhausts for his dyno engine.

Most 400-cubic-inch RHS circle track small-blocks are outfitted with Brodix aluminum cylinder heads. These heads have significantly larger intake and exhaust runners than cast iron Chevy street heads. Scooter wondered whether a 400-cubic-inch street small-block would respond to the alloy heads' airflow improvement. The RHS cylinder head department prepared a pair of -10 Brodix castings with 200cc intake runners for Scooter's dyno tests. Scooter calculated that the Brodix heads' small 64cc combustion chambers would raise the engine's compression ratio to 11.6:1.

CAMSHAFT CHOICES

It's just a short walk across the street from Racing Head Service to Competition Cams, so Scooter had no shortage of cams to try in his 400-cubic-inch small-block. In fact, he tested the entire range of Competition Cams' Magnum series of high-performance hydraulic cams. Today's hydraulic cam profiles rival the performance of solid lifter grinds, but without the clatter of mechanical lifters and the hassles of frequent valve adjustments. Once the dyno tests were underway, Scooter quickly discovered that the 400-cubic-inch small-block is very responsive to camshaft timing. A Competition Cams 280 Magnum (230-degree duration at .050-inch tappet lift, .480-inch valve lift) produced a baseline reading of 410 horsepower at 5000 rpm with the cast iron Chevy heads.

Switching to the high-compression Brodix aluminum heads increased the maximum power reading to 450 horsepower. Substituting a 292 Magnum (244-degree duration, .501-inch lift) boosted the power level to 438 horsepower with the iron heads, and 480 horsepower with the aluminum castings. Scooter saved the best for last, though. In his final series of dyno runs with a 305 Magnum (253-degree duration, .525-inch lift), the 400-cubic-inch

small-block pumped out an astonishing 453 horsepower with the Chevy heads. Bolting on the Brodix castings produced a phenomenal peak power reading of 506 horsepower!

Any street engine that produces over 500 horsepower with flat-top pistons and an hydraulic must be taken seriously. The 400-cubic-inch small-block is lighter, smaller, cheaper, and more reliable at high rpm than a big-block V8 and, as Scooter demonstrated, it can rival the rat motor for sheer horsepower.

As impatient youngsters, we are constantly admonished to remember that good things come in small packages. In the case of a 400-cubic-inch small-block, that advice is certainly appropriate. It takes a sharp eye to spot the difference between a milquetoast 283 and a bruising 400-cubic-inch V8. That's part of the appeal of Chevrolet's unknown performance engine. But thanks to the efforts of engine builders like Scooter Brothers, the 400's days of anonymity are over.

CONTINUED FROM PAGE 25

shotpeening (rod and cap). Also available are the factory heat-treated 302 rods in both the 2.000 inch and 2.100 inch sizes (5.703 inches long). CSC's forged chrome-moly rods can be had in three lengths: 5.703; 5.850; and 6.000 inches – all in either 2.000 or 2-1/16 inch pin sizes. The forged aluminum rods come in either 5.703 or 6.000 inch lengths.

The CSC forged pistons are available in a full range of bore sizes from stock to 0.030 inches over, (0.060 over on special order) and pin heights ranging from 1.800 to 1.250 inches, as measured from the center of the pin to deck of the piston. Both flat tops and the CSC "Fire-Slot" design domes are available (figures 7 and 8), and both can be made to take advantage of a unique ring design made possible for the small-block engine by the 400's larger bore size. Called "head-land" rings, they are placed in the top ring groove which is cut just below the piston's deck surface (figures 8 and 9). The ring is of a dykes design; high ring placement fully exposes the ring to the pressure in the cylinder, making it work more effectively. It has not been possible to use the step-land design with some of the smaller bore Chevy pistons because the valve clearance notches were placed so close to the piston edge that the high, top-ring groove cut through into the clearance notch. The 400 incher's pistons have enough material around the outside of the piston to cut a satisfactory ring groove without worrying about cutting into the valve notch. A coil expander keeps tension on the dykes ring, forcing it against the cylinder wall to keep a good seal at low rpm.

Chevrolet obviously does not *need* a high performance small-block engine in the 400 cubic inch range, because everything that is wrong with the small-block 400 from a performance angle, is right with their 396 or 400 inch big-block "Rat" motor. Even weight is not a factor when you consider that the ZL-1's aluminum block is now readily available – if you have the *price*. But the basic design of the small-block has been around long enough that there is a ton of equipment, new and used, just waiting to be bolted to a 400 block, be it stock, stroked or destroked. For a non-performance engine, this one is bound to run! ©

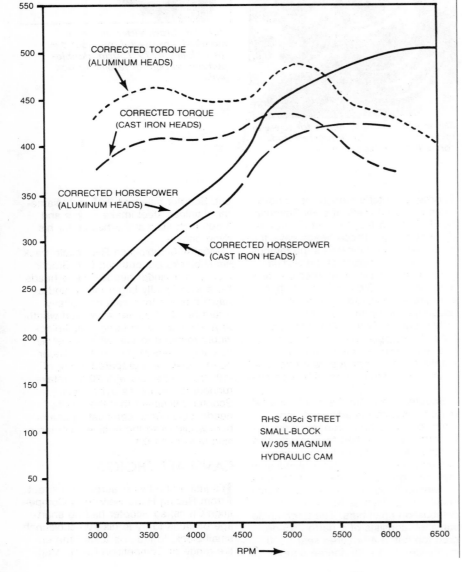

CORRECTED TORQUE
(ALUMINUM HEADS)

CORRECTED TORQUE
(CAST IRON HEADS)

CORRECTED HORSEPOWER
(ALUMINUM HEADS)

CORRECTED HORSEPOWER
(CAST IRON HEADS)

RHS 405ci STREET
SMALL-BLOCK
W/305 MAGNUM
HYDRAULIC CAM

RPM ➤

"Well, it saved me the price of a paint job . . ."

BUILT TO STAY TOUGH

By David Vizard

This Nitrous Small-Block Chevy Has Bottom-End Punch and High-Speed Power

The original concept of this project was to see just how much power could be extracted from a *totally streetable* engine. This meant that the engine's power curve must suit the characteristics of a stock torque converter and the engine must be able to live on currently available low-octane gas, it must get reasonable gas mileage under normal driving conditions, and it must be able to withstand the rigors of the added horsepower from nitrous oxide injection.

The project culminated with almost a solid month of dyno tests on an advanced Superflow SF 800 computerized dyno. In order to get just the right combination of parts, we tested three carbs, four types of spacers, three nitrous oxide kits, four intake manifolds, two types of headers (in four different configurations), two valvetrains, and several different air cleaner assemblies. The end result was an engine comprised of hand-picked components that worked well together. This ultimate nitrous-oxide injected, small-block Chevy engine averages 25 mpg (highway) and can push a 3800-pound car down the quarter in the mid 11s.

Building The Bottom End

Block—The basis of our engine was a 350-cubic-inch, four-bolt main, small-block Chevy. The block was stripped down, all the major core plugs and oil galley plugs were removed, and then the bare block was hot-tanked. After this it was bored .030-inch over and honed to the finished size required by the piston-type used. Honing was done with a deck plate to ensure the block had bores as round as possible in its loaded condition. All the machine work on the block was done by Steve Clif-

This Sealed Power piston has relatively little pop-up, but is still good for 10.5:1 compression when 67cc chambers are used.

ton's B&D Auto Machine in Tucson, Arizona.

Pistons—Forged, Sealed Power pistons, giving 10.5:1 compression (with 67cc combustion chambers in the heads) were used. The ring packs selected to go with them were for a .035-inch oversize bore. This allowed the rings to be gapped exactly as per the specifications contained in the piston installation instructions. Nothing trick was done on the piston-to-bore clearance. The final sizing on the bores produced the clearances specified in the piston installation instructions.

Rods—Since this engine was ex-

pected to take quite a beating, considerable attention was paid to preparation of the connecting rods. A reasonably matched set of eight rods was selected from about a hundred rods. We looked for large balance pads on the wrist pin end of the rod. We also wanted a good match between the two halves of the forging (good beam alignment), so that when the flash was removed, the beam cleaned up without too much metal being carved off. Another important factor was a cleanly machined radius where the bolt head goes.

(continued overleaf)

Nitrous Small-Block

After selecting the rods, we numbered each rod to its cap, arbitrarily 1-8. The bolts were then removed from each rod and the beams cleaned up by grinding in a longitudinal direction (up and down the rod) so there would be no flaws running across the rod which might grow into a crack. The balance pads on the wrist pin end were reduced, but enough metal remained for the final balancing operation. The radius corner of the bolt head face was polished to remove all flaws visible to the naked eye. At this point, the rods were sent off to be Tufftrided. This was an important operation on our engine because the rods will take a beating. Tufftriding can increase the fatigue resistance of the rods by at least 30 percent.

When the rods came back from being Tufftrided, they began their reconditioning procedure. This was done at Motor Machine & Supply, Tucson, Arizona. The first step was to match up all the rod caps with the top half of the rod, and then grind the split-line on each rod and cap. (Many rod conditioning companies grind the cap at a slight angle so that when the bolts are installed and tightened, it pulls the sides of the rod in slightly so that when the rod journal bore is honed, it cleans up its entire 360° circumference. This practice must not be done on a rod intended for high-performance use, as it leads to fatiguing in the rod bolt head face radius; that's the one that was polished earlier on. This practice also reduces the fatigue life of the rod bolt.) The rod cap actually needs to be ground at a slight angle so that tightening the rod bolts causes the cap to spread fractionally at the split-line. The angle needs to be only enough to cause the rod to spread about .001-inch at the split-line.

Once the caps and rods have been cut, the rod is assembled using SPS rod bolts, and the rod nuts are torqued to 50 ft.-lbs. At this point, the rod honing machine bore gauge is set up to read the required size. The rod is then put into a C-clamp, and the sides of the rod are pulled in to remove the .001-inch spread. While held in this clamp, the rod is then honed to its bottom limit with a coarse honing stone. The reason for the coarse finish and the tight sizing on the rod journal bore is to hold the bearing tightly in place under heavy loads, such as nitrous oxide injection. Should the engine detonate, these modifications should markedly reduce the possibility of bearing spin.

Crank—This was next on the list of items to prepare, and the work was done with due reference to the work performed on the con rod journal bores. Because the rods are holding the bearings tight, clearance between bearing and crank can be reduced. When the

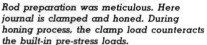

Rod preparation was meticulous. Here journal is clamped and honed. During honing process, the clamp load counteracts the built-in pre-stress loads.

crank was ground by Jerry Nelson (whose crank shop is in the back of Ron's Place in Tucson, Arizona), it was sized to the bottom limit of a -.010 regrind. Not only were the journals accurately sized, but attention was also paid to the corner fillet radius to limit the amount of stress at this point. Finally, the crank was polished and then passed along (plus the rods and pistons, damper, and flexplate) to Ronnie Upham at Ron's Place for balancing.

Balancing—Due to the fact that the lightening operation, plus slightly lighter pistons, had resulted in the reciprocating weight being reduced by some 50 grams, a considerable amount of metal had to come off the crank counterweights in order to get the crank balanced.

Assembly—The bottom-end assembly followed normal procedure. Federal Mogul bearings were used throughout, and the rods were torqued to the 50 ft.-lbs. specified for SPS bolts. A trial assembly was made without rings to check the deck-to-piston clearance. During this assembly, push-fit piston pins were used so that the pistons and rods could be juggled around to give the most consistent piston-to-deck height. After the trial assembly, a light decking operation was done on both decks to bring the piston-to-deck height to a nominal .010-inch below the deck.

Cam & Valvetrain

For this particular project, it was decided that radical cam changes would only be done as a last resort, so a cam with known qualities under a variety of different conditions was chosen—the Competition Cams 268-H. The drive for the cam from the crank was by a semi-roller truck chain. This is not a true roller chain, but for our purposes, it is more than adequate, and it's a lot cheaper than most true roller chains. The cam was timed per the Competition Cams spec sheet.

Lifters, rockers, retainers, and valve springs were also supplied by Competition Cams. The rockers that were found to work best on the engine were 1.6:1-ratio items. To avoid valve float at this engine's full rpm (6500 rpm), some fairly heavy valve springs were necessary. The springs were shimmed to give 110 pounds of valve spring tension on the seat, and at full lift (0.474-inch), 260 pounds. The pushrods used were *selected* TRW chrome-moly items. The pushrods must be absolutely straight. A bowed or bent pushrod would not only give bad valve action, but will inevitably fail. On the other hand, a good, straight, chrome-moly pushrod is approximately twice as stiff as a standard out-of-the-box Chevy item.

Topping off the valvetrain was a Moroso single-rail, U-bolt-type stud girdle. This was deemed necessary in view of the 1.6:1-ratio rockers and the relatively heavy spring loads used. The 1.6:1 rockers produced quite a bit of valve lift in relation to the short timing of the cam, so it was reckoned that the valvetrain could stand some stiffening up. To use the Moroso stud girdle, it was necessary to use the Moroso rocker covers, as added internal clearance is necessary when this valvetrain combination is used.

Cylinder Heads

While the engine was still in the planning stage, much work was done

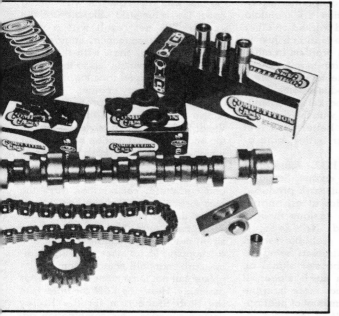

This is the cam and valvetrain kit as it came from Competition Cams. The only change made was the replacement of the chain and gears shown here with roller-type truck items, mainly because of the lengthy dyno session.

Here's how the valvetrain looks just prior to finishing. To adjust the valve lash, the U-bolts are slackened off, the large screw is then adjusted, and the U-bolts are retightened.

on cylinder heads by Carl Schattilly of C&G Porting (Tucson, Arizona, 602/323-1578). The easiest route for the cylinder heads would have been to put on a set of Carl's $1000 super street heads. These heads flow about as well as a typical set of Pro Stock heads, which cost usually half as much again. However, outright horsepower was not the only criterion. A set of well-ported 292 turbo heads only offers advantages in areas which our engine could not take advantage of. For instance, 292 heads showed substantial gains in airflow over other types of Chevy heads in valve lifts above about .500-inch. The project engine would be using a cam with less than .500-inch lift. 292 heads also tend to be at their best when used with compression ratios of 11.5 or more, and at rpm a little above where the project engine is expected to peak. Without a doubt, a 292 turbo head suitably modified would be superior as far as horsepower is concerned in comparison with other modified Chevy head castings, but this is only important if the vehicle is to be an out-and-out race machine. This particular project engine had to get good mileage, and this meant it would spend a lot of time operating between 1000 and 2000 rpm on light throttle. The indications from previous test engines are that a fully modified 292 head will not show results as good as alternative castings, suitably modified.

Intake Port—To get the best low-end horsepower, responsiveness, and part-throttle economy, together with a good amount of top-end horsepower, we needed an intake port which flowed well (especially in the lower lift ranges), had good port velocity, and had a minimum amount of volume consistent with the airflow required. The tradeoff between port velocity and total flow was done on a simple basis of average port velocity in feet per second times the cfm airflow at 25 inches of water pressure drop. Using this criteria, a trapezoidal port shape was developed which also had only a minimal amount of metal out of the port in the pocket area. The whole port was finished with a coarse stone to reduce the effect of fuel puddling. The only area polished was that immediately adjacent to the valve seat. Both the valve seats in the head and on the valve received a great deal of attention to promote good flow right off the valve seat.

The last factor of any importance is that both 1.94 and 2.02-inch intake valves were tried (the larger were ultimately installed). The final results showed that there was little or no difference between these valves, over the lift ranges we were interested in.

Exhaust Port—In order to get good economy from an engine, it is imperative that the exhaust has as free an exit as possible to reduce the pumping losses of an engine to a minimum. With this in mind, the exhaust port was given a full Pro Stock-type treatment, together with 1.6-inch valves. From previous testing, it was also known what sort of exhaust manifold size was going to be needed, so the head was matched up to some header plates.

Apart from the flow work on the cylinder heads, attention was paid to the valve guides and oil stem seals. Here, K-Line bronze guides were used together with the K-Line stem seals. The importance of good wear-resistant guides and effective oil stem seals on this engine cannot be overemphasized. To effectively use a 10.5:1 compression ratio means that there is no margin for octane reduction because of oil contamination due to oil passing down the guides. Also, heavy springs and rapid valve opening rates tend to wear guides faster than normal. The bronze guides plus the easing of side loads due to use of roller rockers are there to maintain the level of performance.

Once all the porting and machine work had been done, the heads were cc'd and surfaced to give the desired 10.5:1 compression ratio.

Carbs & Manifolds

Quite a few carb and manifold combinations were flushed over the flow bench in conjunction with heads that were intended for use on the engine. This range of manifolds included the stock two-plane, 180°, cast-iron Chevy intake manifold. The stock unit was included in this test because many previous tests had shown it was a good mileage manifold to be used as a standard by which to judge alternative manifolds.

After some initial dyno testing on the engine, it was decided to stick with one of two carbs, a stock 650 Holley or a 730-cfm Internal Combustion Engineering (602/889-2779) modified 650 Holley. Basically the 730-cfm I.C.E. Holley is a radically modified 650 Holley. The extra airflow is achieved by modifying the

(continued overleaf)

Nitrous Small-Block

venturis, the boosters, and the butterflies. On the dyno model, the choke horn has been machined off and surfaces blended into the venturis. However, if you should buy one of these, the latest I.C.E. version of this carb retains the choke mechanism in its entirety and uses the new, K&N Stub Stack, as this unit achieves the same airflow as machining off the choke assembly. The carb retains all the requirements of a good street carb, plus it inherits the performance potential of a race carb.

Headers

The headers selected for this engine were 1¾-inch-diameter primary, both in anti-reversion and non-anti-reversion configurations. Both headers were from Cyclone.

Dyno Tests

During the dyno tests, many important facts concerning intake manifolds, carbs, and exhausts were discovered. The first intake manifold tried, a 360° open-plenum type, together with the stock Holley carb, gave poor results,

due mainly to a fuel distribution problem. In this application the manifold didn't work out. It had worked on other engines, but this time it didn't. Just to check that it wasn't a problem in other areas, a stock, cast-iron manifold was installed on the engine, together with a stock Holley. This produces some 20 hp more than the aftermarket 360° manifold. Fuel distribution with the cast-iron manifold was much better, and fuel consumption was far better, both at part and full throttle.

At this point, the I.C.E. 730 Holley was bolted on to the engine. Economy testing showed that this carb produced better brake specifics at all engine speeds and all the various throttle openings checked. However, it dropped 14 hp. The probable reason for this was the fuel droplets being too small. Because the booster signal on this I.C.E. carb was much higher, it broke up the fuel much more than the stock carb. With the amount of heat applied to the underside of the stock intake manifold, this finely atomized fuel was turning into a vapor, which, of course, caused it to expand, and this caused the air consumption of the engine to drop. In other words, because

the fuel was vaporizing, it was cutting down the volumetric efficiency of the engine. The net result was a very smooth, crisp, economical engine with less horsepower than with the stock carb. This observation led to the exploration of non-heated race manifolds for use on the economy engine.

A manifold that had proved very effective in the past was the Edelbrock Victor Junior, which finally ended up on the engine. A combination of the Victor Junior plus the I.C.E. carb resulted in exceptionally good part-throttle fuel economy figures. Plus, this manifold and carburetor combination gave the best torque curve and the best horsepower figures of all the combinations: 31 hp more than the best stock carb/street manifold combination tried, and a whopping 65 hp more than the original carb/manifold combination.

Last but not least comes the air filter assembly. Here, the K&N air filter with the Stub Stack ram for the Holley proved superior. This combination actually gave a good, solid 7 hp more than could be obtained with an open intake. More power and clean air equates to an engine which will last a lot longer as well as go quicker.

As far as valve gear, the 1.6 rockers were selected because they improved the top-end hp. The difference between 1.5 and 1.6 roller rockers was virtually zero until about 4000 rpm, at which point, the two power curves started to diverge. At 6000 rpm there was some 17 hp difference.

Exhaust—The final specification for the exhaust ran something like this: Cyclone 1¾-inch primary A.R. headers with a cross-over pipe just aft of the collector. The exhaust exited through two turbo mufflers. When testing the various exhaust systems, two things became apparent. To make the A.R. work successfully, a cross-over pipe must be installed. Although the cross-over pipe helped with a non-A.R. system, the A.R. system proved to be worse on the engine than a non-A.R. system until the cross-over pipe was added; then it showed its superiority. Also, the cross-over pipe helped mid-range torque on this particular engine. With the engine spec as per Fig. 1, and the ignition timing set to 36° full advance, the engine pulled, in complete street form (with mufflers and air filter on, plus a diet of 91-octane fuel), the power curve shown in Fig. 2. The engine would take full load, full throttle cleanly from 800 to 6500 rpm. At 6500 the power was down, but at 6000 it was still putting out a healthy 372 hp. Peak horsepower in this totally street form was 376, and peak torque was 404 ft.-lbs. That is the sort of torque output you would expect from an engine with a few more cubic inches than this one has.

Assuming the car's gearing and

FIG. 1

Engine

Block:	350 4-bolt, bored .030 over
Pistons:	Sealed Power 7051P (.030 over)
Rings:	Sealed Power R9343 (.035 over)
Rods:	Tufftrided & lightened as per text
Rod Bolts:	SPS
Crank:	Ground .010/.010 & Tufftrided
Bearings:	Federal Mogul
Timing Chain & Gears:	Chevy 350, truck
Oil Pump:	Melling, high volume
Dampener:	Stock 350
Piston to Bore Clearance:	.0035/.004
Deck Height:	.010-.013
Cam:	Competition Cams 268H
Lifters:	Sealed Power HT 817R
Pushrods:	TRW chrome-moly
Rockers:	1.6:1
Retainers & Springs:	1.5-inch NASCAR-type springs & Super Loc retainers

Cylinder Heads

186 castings reworked by C&G Porting.
High-flow/high-velocity trapezoidal intake port, 2.02 valve.
Pro Stock exhaust port with matched header plate, 1.6 valve.
Chamber volume, nominal 67cc.
Intake manifold: Edelbrock, Victor Junior.
Carburetor: 730-cfm I.C.E. unit, based on 650 Holley.
Headers: Cyclone 1¾-inch A.R. with cross-over pipe.

Nitrous Oxide Injection System

(All the following produced virtually the same results.)

N.O.S.—Double spray bar street system
I.C.E.—Double spray bar street system
10,000 RPM—Stage II, 4-hole spacer, triple spray bar

Nitrous Small-Block

chassis are up to it, the engine in this form has enough horsepower to push a typical Z28 down the strip in around 13.5 seconds, which is good, but 11 was promised. Enter the nitrous oxide.

Nitrous Oxide Injection

It's quite apparent from the power figures that our project engine has more than enough power for ordinary day-to-day driving. Also, when checked out at steady speeds on a road-load curve for a Camaro, the fuel consumption worked out to around 25-26 mpg at 55-60 mph.

The icing on the cake is the nitrous oxide injection. Three nitrous oxide systems were deemed suitable for this engine: a street Nitrous Oxide Systems kit (213/595-7074), a spray-bar I.C.E. kit and a Stage II 10,000 RPM kit (213/325-8848). The first two kits employed ½-inch spacers. The third kit employed a 1¾-inch spacer. Although all these systems worked well and gave almost identical results as far as torque and power are concerned, it was decided to use either the I.C.E. system or the N.O.S. system as they utilized ½-inch spacers. (The vehicle the engine was going into would have a hood clearance problem if the 1¾-inch 10,000 RPM kit had been used together with the much higher Victor Junior manifold.)

As far as choosing between the N.O.S. and I.C.E. systems, the choice falls to the individual. The I.C.E. system is less expensive than the N.O.S. system by some $30 and is more compact, but the N.O.S. system makes slightly more efficient use of the nitrous oxide consumed; you could make an extra pass, or maybe even two, down the strip before emptying the bottle.

With the mufflers still in place, and running on 92-octane gas, the nitrous oxide-injected engine produced 491 hp at 5150 rpm and a whopping 562 ft.-lbs. of torque at 4100 rpm. Gearing permitting, this engine now had enough beans to push a Z28 down the strip in the low 12s or high 11s, but we're not finished yet.

The next move was to change over from premium pump fuel to So-Cal Orange racing fuel. The results were very worthwhile. Basically, with the So-Cal Orange, the timing set to 39-40 degrees, and the headers uncorked, the engine produced 414 hp at 5500 rpm. Along with this came a peak torque of 412 ft.-lbs. at 4250 rpm. Planting nitrous fairly and squarely into this engine bumped the uncorked, race-gased horsepower up to 529 with a peak torque of 570 ft.-lbs. Just for the record, if you can get that much torque and horsepower to the ground, you can put almost anything into the 11s. **HR**

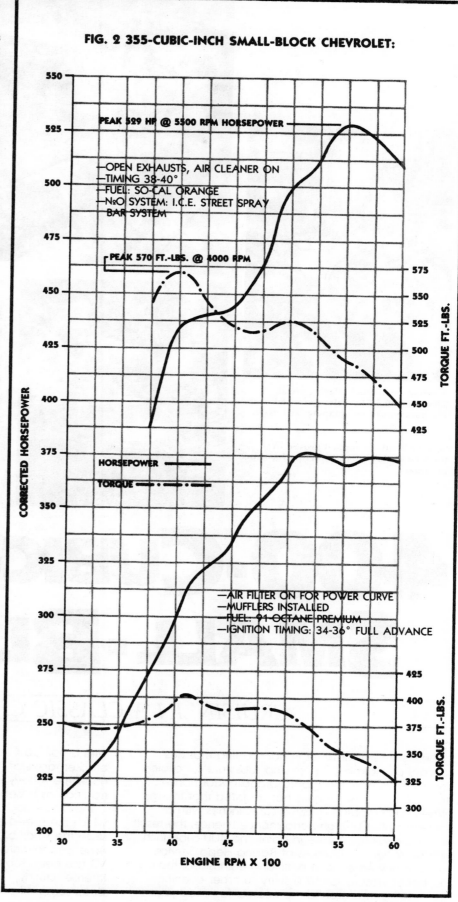

FIG. 2 355-CUBIC-INCH SMALL-BLOCK CHEVROLET:

PEAK 529 HP @ 5500 RPM HORSEPOWER

OPEN EXHAUSTS, AIR CLEANER ON
TIMING 38-40°
FUEL: SO-CAL ORANGE
N₂O SYSTEM: I.C.E. STREET SPRAY BAR SYSTEM

PEAK 570 FT.-LBS. @ 4000 RPM

HORSEPOWER
TORQUE

AIR FILTER ON FOR POWER CURVE
MUFFLERS INSTALLED
FUEL: 91-OCTANE PREMIUM
IGNITION TIMING: 34-36° FULL ADVANCE

CORRECTED HORSEPOWER

TORQUE FT.-LBS.

ENGINE RPM X 100

A prime small-block: Racing Head Service's 400ci Chevrolet produced over 450 horsepower on computerized dyno.

Scooter Brothers applied proven oval track technology to his street performance program.

400ci Chevrolet V8 is the big brother of the small-block. It has huge 4.125-inch cylinder bores, yet retains the same external dimensions as original 265ci V8s.

400-CUBIC-INCH SMALL-BLOCK

CRUISIN' IN A CLASSIC CHEVY

There's a familiar tenet in hot rodding that has always proclaimed, "There's no substitute for cubic inches." But, now the supercharged performance technology of the Eighties has negated that truism: When you combine massive cubic inches with a generous shot of high-performance science, the result is overpowering. A case in point: the 400-cubic-inch, 450hp *street* small-blocks of Racing Head Service.

For many Americana buffs and enthusiasts, there's no better way to spend a sultry summer evening than doing laps around the nearest fast-food joint with a hot '56 Chevy, or proclaiming the king of the bracket racers at the local dragstrip. The classic mid-Fifties Chevy is as much a part of the American tradition as baseball, apple pie and senior proms.

The small-block Chevrolet V8 is the foundation on which the speed equipment industry is built. Ever since the small-block dethroned the flathead as America's favorite performance engine, Chevy's little V8 has been subjected to the aftermarket's most intense scrutiny. From high-rise manifolds to deep-sump oil pans, from solid lifter camshafts to

RHS selects blocks with four-bolt main bearing caps for high-performance applications. 400ci block has unusual 2.650-inch main bearings.

Cast iron 400 crankshaft has excellent durability in high-output street engine, thanks to large main journal diameter.

400 blocks have siamesed cylinder walls to accommodate large-diameter cylinder bores. Steam holes in deck surface aid coolant flow; water does not circulate between adjacent cylinders.

cavernous carburetors, the small-block Chevrolet has captured the majority of speed equipment sales since its introduction 30 years ago.

With a few exceptions, the evolution of street performance small-blocks has been haphazard. Pro Chevy racers could rely on engine dynos and lap times to gauge their progress, but street enthusiasts monitored their efforts by the seat of their pants and the whine of sirens. Now, however, engine-building techniques that were reserved for all-out racing engines are available for serious street motors. With computer-designed cam profiles, flow-tested cylinder heads and development time on automated dynamometers, today's street performance small-block has the pedigree of a thoroughbred competition engine.

The ultra-performance small-blocks under development by Racing Head Service in Memphis, Tennessee, are a perfect example of this New Age street engine building. With 17 years of experience building Chevrolet engines for drag racing and oval track competition, RHS has recently embarked on an ambitious program of marketing ''mail-order horsepower.'' The task of developing a powerful, reliable and affordable street small-block fell to Scooter Brothers. Scooter is a walking definition of a car enthusiast: 40-weight racing oil courses through his veins and developing an ultra-performance Chevrolet was a challenge he just couldn't resist.

In addition to enthusiasm, Scooter brought to the

project considerable experience with large-displacement small-blocks. An avid fan of dirt track racing, Scooter has watched the 400-cubic-inch small-block Chevrolet V8 become the standard powerplant in unlimited oval track racing. In Late Model Sportsman classes these big small-blocks dominate. Throttle response, torque and reliability are the most important characteristics an engine can have—exactly the qualities demanded by a strong street Chevy. Rather than using the exotic, expensive components required for weekly competition on the ovals, Scooter knew that carefully selected production Chevrolet components offered all the dependability and horsepower he needed.

Because even a maximum-effort street engine must cope with traffic jams and service station gasoline, a 400-cubic-inch small-block was Scooter's logical starting point. The extra inches of Chevrolet's biggest small-block allow an engine builder to bolt together a relatively mild engine combination. Instead of relying on a radical cam profile, multiple carburetion and an extreme compression ratio, Scooter's streetworthy small-block relies on vast piston displacement for its performance.

The 400-cubic-inch small-block Chevrolet V8 is enjoying a tremendous surge in popularity. Originally released in 1970 for use in sedans, station wagons and trucks, it was overlooked by Chevrolet performance enthusiasts for a decade. A High Output version of the 400 was never an assembly-line

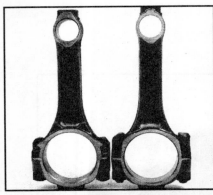

Stock 400 rod (left) has short rod bolts, 5.565-inch center-to-center length. Scooter uses 5.700-inch-long 350-type rods with high-strength fasteners in his high-performance 400s.

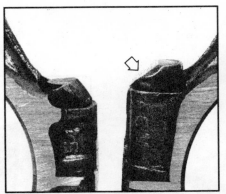

Rod bolt head must be chamfered for cam clearance when 350 rod is used with long-stroke 400 crank.

RHS replaces dished cast aluminum 400 piston with flat-top Venolia forged aluminum piston. Aftermarket piston increases compression to 10.6:1 and has higher wrist pin hole to accommodate long 350-type connecting rods.

Scooter selected early-Seventies cylinder head castings with large 73cc combustion chambers for his ultra-performance 400ci small-block. Holes are drilled in head to match steam holes in block.

option, so the engine lacked the performance reputation of its small-block siblings. Its cast-iron crankshaft and short connecting rods were regarded as liabilities by the street machine set.

What its opponents overlooked, however, is that the 400 is still a small-block. With a displacement 50-percent larger than the original 265-cubic-inch V8 that made its debut in 1955, the 400 retains all the external dimensions of every other small-block and enjoys unlimited parts interchangeability with other small-blocks. It took a while for street machine enthusiasts to recognize the potential of the 400 small-block, but it has become the engine of choice on Main Street, U.S.A.

The basis of Scooter's street engine program is a well-seasoned 400 block. In view of the projected power levels, he chose a block with four-bolt main bearing caps. The 400 is something of a maverick among small-blocks, as it is the only one with 2.650-inch-diameter main bearings. (All other small-blocks built since 1969 have 2.450-inch main bearings.) Its 4.125-inch-diameter cylinders are the largest in any production small-block. Its bores are so big that the walls of adjacent cylinders actually join;

no water circulates between these siamesed cylinders. Because Scooter selected a used block to keep costs low, the case was carefully inspected with magnetic powder for cracks, then its cylinders were overbored .030-inch. Surfacing the decks ensured they were parallel to the crankshaft centerline.

All production crankshafts for 400-cubic-inch small-blocks have a stroke of 3.750 inches, and are made of cast nodular iron. Scooter has found these stock cranks perfectly satisfactory for heavy-duty street performance use. The generous diameter of the main bearing journals certainly contributes to the crankshaft's surprising strength. Crank preparation is straightforward: The core is Magnaflux-inspected, then the rod and main journals are reground and micropolished.

Scooter substitutes connecting rods from a 350-cubic-inch small-block for the stock 400 rods which are .135-inch shorter than all other small-block rods (5.565-inch center-to-center length vs. 5.700-inch), and also use shorter through bolts. Scooter finds the 350-style rod more reliable in a high-performance application, and its longer center-to-center dimension improves the rod

Sharp edges in intake valve bowl are carefully blended; exhaust runner is fully ported. RHS grinds three-angle valve seats, leaves combustion chamber stock.

400ci small-block is externally balanced, requires custom counterweighted converter flexplate and harmonic balancer.

Aftermarket flywheel is drilled for proper balance for 400 crankshaft.

CHEVROLET PERFORMANCE: 1956 CHEVY STREET MACHINE

Competition Cams valvetrain includes Magnum roller tip rocker arms (1.52:1 ratio), steel retainers and stock diameter high-performance valve springs.

angularity. RHS uses selected 350 rod cores, which are inspected, shotpeened and resized. The only modification required to install the 350 rods in a 400-cubic-inch small-block is to slightly bevel several bolt heads for camshaft clearance. Since the 400 and 350 connecting rods share a 2.100-inch journal diameter, standard Clevite small-block inserts are used.

On the street and the racetrack, adequate engine airflow is essential to performance. There's no lack of expertise with cylinder head ports at Racing Head Service, so Scooter's men in the grinding room prepared a set of early-Seventies heads (casting No. 441) for his development engine. These heads have the same generous runners as the famous "fuel injection" heads of the Sixties, and also possess large 76cc combustion chambers. This feature is important because it keeps the compression ratio down to a reasonable level despite the 400's enormous cylinder volume. With flat-top Venolia pistons, the final compression ratio is a moderate 10.6:1.

The intake side of the cylinder heads requires only a simple cleanup and blending operation in the valve bowl. Three-angle valve seats are ground for the 2.02-inch intake and 1.60-inch exhaust valves. Because exhaust flow is critical in these large-displacement small-blocks, the exhaust port is completely ported and polished.

Scooter has found the 400-cubic-inch small-block quite responsive to camshaft timing. A series of dyno tests with progressively larger Competition Cams hydraulic cam grinds proved fruitful. A Competition Cams 280 Magnum (230-degrees duration at .050-inch tappet lift) produced a baseline of 410 horsepower at 5000 rpm. Substituting a 292 Magnum boosted the power level to 438 horsepower; bolting in a 305 Magnum yielded an astonishing 453 horsepower at 5500 rpm!

Impatient youngsters are advised that good things come in small packages. In the case of a 400-cubic-inch small-block, that advice is certainly accurate. It takes a sharp eye to spot the difference between a milquetoast 283 and a bruising 400-cubic-inch V8. That's part of the appeal of Chevrolet's unknown performance engine. But thanks to the efforts of engine builders such as Scooter Brothers, the 400's days of anonymity have come to an end. □

HAND-ME-DOWN

HORSEPOWER

MODERNIZING THE LT-1 350 FOR THE EIGHTIES

The year was 1971. One day in February, Jim Redding Sr. joined the ranks of those who recognized that the musclecar era was in decline. The telltale signs were evident. In the sales brochures, the variety of real performance options was dwindling. The factory engineers had their fun through the Sixties but by the end of the decade a new awareness was growing. The public began to see the automobile as the chief source of air pollution and began pressuring lawmakers to do something about it, resulting in laws that required new cars to pass strict emissions tests at the time of manufacture. In order to pass the tests, overall power and performance suffered a great deal.

Jim Sr. knew that in another year there might not be much to choose from in the way of hard-core performance, so he went to his local Chevrolet dealer and ordered a Z28 just the way he wanted it—a basic sport coupe with an LT-1 350 V8 and an automatic transmission. The four-speed manual gearbox was no longer available in California and, as a consequence, the 12-bolt rearend was deemed not necessary by the factory people and was also no longer available. However, the 4.10 limited-slip rearend and the Turbo 400 automatic were available on a special-order basis.

The '71 Camaro was more performance-oriented than the years that followed but not quite as muscular as the years that preceded it. Feeling a little nostalgic for the musclecar era, Jim Sr. changed the intake manifold and carburetor when the car was less than a year old. Off came the factory aluminum high-rise and 780cfm vacuum-secondary Hol-

ley, and on went an Edelbrock TM-1 Tarantula and 800cfm double-pumper mechanical-secondary Holley. A set of Hooker headers and a 3000rpm stall-speed torque converter were installed at the same time. These changes kept the performance-restless spirit inside Jim Sr. quiet for about five years until, in early 1977, more changes took place.

A complete engine rebuild with more breathing capacity in mind resulted in the replacement of the LT-1 cylinder heads with angle-plug 292 Turbo castings. The new camshaft came from the Chevrolet high-performance parts list, No. 3927140 solid lifter, with .050-inch duration numbers of 243 degrees intake and 254 degrees exhaust. The pistons were changed to 11.0:1 forged TRWs. At the time these modifications were done, premium gas was still available. The car was

1 The Speed-Pro pistons are measured across the skirts to determine the exact amount of clearance necessary.

2 This measurement is written directly on top of the piston so it can be compared to all the others and to ensure that all pistons are the correct size.

3 With the block secured by the main saddles, the boring bar cuts exactly perpendicular to the centerline of the crankshaft.

4 A Sunnen CK-10 is used to hone the taper of the bores to within .0001 inch. The final honing is done with a fine finish for the moly rings.

5 The combustion chambers are enlarged slightly on the computer-controlled mill at AirFlow Research Cylinder Heads. This gives an additional 5cc so the compression ratio is a streetable 9.5:1.

more powerful than before but the drive-ability had diminished to barely tolerable.

The end of the Seventies brought high prices at the fuel pumps with a proportional decrease in octane numbers that left high-compression engine owners in line at the local speed shop for fuel additives and octane boosters. The Camaro, being sensitive to low octane, began to feel the pain of detonation. In just a few short years the LT-1 sadly expired, the pistons no longer able to withstand the crushing pressures of two colliding flame fronts. They crumbled and fell helpless into the oil pan. With the proud small-block silent, the car was retired to the left side of the driveway, only a ghost of what once was.

Several years later, 18-year-old Jim Redding Jr. was looking for a direction to take in college. Having grown up in and around his dad's Camaro, he inherited the performance spirit and decided to become an engineer with a specialization in the automotive environment. He enrolled in the automotive courses at Chaffey College in Alta Loma, California, to learn what it takes to create performance the right way. At the same time, Dad turned the Camaro over to Jim Jr. to help him on his way.

Part of Jim's education at Chaffey is an engine blueprinting class in which, during

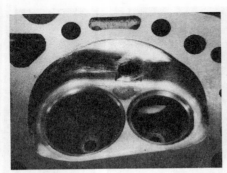

6 AirFlow smooths over the rough edges left from the mill and then blends this edge behind the spark plug. Previous dyno tests indicate this is worth some additional power.

9 The Edelbrock cam is being installed with just a light coat of oil for the purpose of degreeing.

7 With all clearances checked and recorded, the short-block assembly now begins.

10 TDC is found prior to degreeing the cam, using a B&B professional degree wheel.

8 Jim carefully torques the B&B rod bolts to 45 ft.-lbs.

eight-hour sessions, he is learning about the sophisticated machinery and processes required to build a precision engine. Naturally the LT-1 is the focal point for Jim, providing a project with personal involvement.

First, the engine was torn down and all the parts inspected. The four-bolt main block survived with some minor scuffing (caused by detonation) and required being bored .060-inch oversize. The connecting rods were Magnafluxed—two of them failed to pass—as were the forged steel crankshaft and the cylinder heads, which did pass. From here, all parts went to the cleaning stage.

This was also a good time to order the new parts. Jim decided on Sealed Power components for most of the internal pieces. In order to cope with the available octane, he needed a 9.5:1 compression ratio, so he chose Sealed Power .060-inch pistons (No. 7064P) along with Speed Pro .065-inch rings (No. R9343) to allow fitting for each bore, thus controlling the ring end gaps. The pistons are flat tops with a single trough-type valve relief. With the piston mocked up in the block, the deck height was .025 inch down from the deck surface and measured 9cc of volume. The cylinder heads were checked and measured 64cc. Along with the .038-inch compressed thickness of the Fel-Pro O-ring-type Teflon head gasket, the compression ratio was 10.1:1, so Jim was faced with the problem of trying to add 5cc of volume to either the deck clearance or the combustion chamber to achieve 9.5:1.

Calling various sources, Jim found that AirFlow Research offers a machining service for turbo castings that involves milling the combustion chambers on a numerically controlled machine to equalize the volumes of the chambers. A by-product of this machining is the addition of 4.5 to 5cc of volume to the chambers, exactly what was needed.

With this problem out of the way the cylinder heads were finished with Sealed Power intake valves (No. V-2054R), exhaust valves (No. V-2051R) and hardened valve keepers (No. VK115R). The

11 The Edelbrock cam and Sealed Power timing chain showed that both were accurate. The intake opening at .050 inch was 10 degrees BTDC, just as the spec card said it should be.

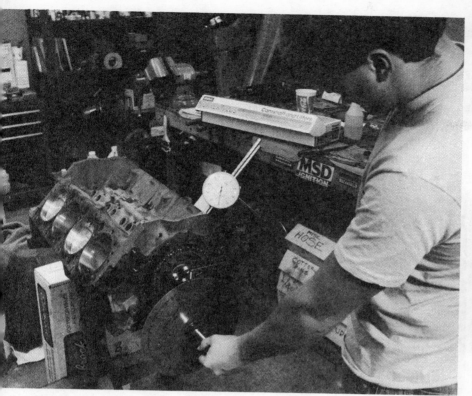

14 Most reputable machine shops will stamp the torque values they used while align-boring the mains so that when you assemble the engine, the main bearing bores will be the same size.

15 Since the oil pump pickup is pressed into the oil pump body, it's necessary to have the pickup heli-arced to prevent it from falling out. The weld doesn't have to encircle the tube—a weld about ¼ inch long will work.

12 Jim checks all the cam specs to determine lobe centers and separation, as well as lobe lift.

13 The Sealed Power intermediate drive-shaft for the oil pump incorporates a steel sleeve instead of a plastic one. The plastic has been known to break and end up in the oil pump.

16 The factory windage tray goes on as the last detail before bolting up the oil pan.

Sealed Power valves feature a one-piece forging for strength and hard, chromed stems for durability, along with a hardened tip to eliminate any need for wear caps. Crane valve springs (No. 99893) were used with Crane retainers (No. 99944) to achieve an installed height of 1.750 inches and a seat pressure of 120 pounds. The full lift pressure is just over 300 pounds. B&B Performance rocker arm studs (No. 3610) replaced the stock ones to improve valvetrain reliability above 5000 rpm. The B&B studs feature a thicker nut and a generous radius where the nut transforms into the threaded portion of the stud.

The connecting rods were prepared by grinding the side of the beams to remove the forging swedge marks. They were then shotpeened by the knowledgeable

TORQUE HORSEPOWER AND VOLUMETRIC EFFICIENCY ACCORDING TO THE X AXIS OF RPM

RPM	Torque	HP	Volumetric Efficiency
2500	310	147	88%
3000	352	201	94%
3500	368	245	97%
4000	375	286	99%
4500	375	322	100%
5000	358	341	100%
5500	341	357	100%
6000	307	351	95%

All figures shown are corrected for 29.92 inches of mercury 60F dry air
91 octane super-unleaded gasoline

17 Using a B&B damper installation tool will save the thrust bearing from being pounded on, as would be the case if a hammer was used to install the damper.

18 A timing tape dramatically increases the readability of the timing marks. This is much more important when the engine is in the car and you're trying to read the timing marks in daylight.

19 This is the Holley 780cfm vacuum-secondary carb that is being reproduced by Holley for restored musclecars from the late Sixties and early Seventies.

people at Polyrock in Chino, California, to restore the surface hardness. They have an automatic machine that uses an intense blast to compact the surface, thereby increasing the surface hardness and reliability of the rods. The rod bolts were replaced with B&B SPS-type bolts (No. 3861) which were resized to exact tolerances with the precision equipment at the college. The crank, rods and pistons were balanced on Stewart-Warner balancing equipment, also at the college.

Bearings for the short-block include rod bearings (No. CB1264P), main bearings (No. MS1523P) and cam bearings (No. SH290S), all from Sealed Power. Bearing clearances are .002-.0025 inch for the rods and .0025-.003 inch for the mains. Piston-to-wall clearance is .005 inch and the rod side clearance is .013-.017 inch.

With all the preliminary measurements taken, the short-block assembly began. Jim chose an Edelbrock Torker-II hydraulic camshaft and lifter set (No. 5002) for the LT-1 for two specific reasons. First, the original camshaft for the LT-1 was a solid lifter-type that possessed .050-inch numbers of 229 degrees intake, 237 degrees exhaust and a lobe separation of 116 degrees; the Edelbrock cam is similar at 232 degrees intake, 234 degrees exhaust and a 108-degree lobe centerline. Second, the Edelbrock Torker-II cam was designed specifically for engines with 9.5:1 compression ratios.

Jim initially ordered Sealed Power long-slot rocker arms (No. R865R) and hardened chromemoly pushrods (No.

RP3212R) but discovered during a trial set-up that the end of the rocker arm slot which is closest to the rocker stud while the lifter is on the base circle interfered with the large radius of the B&B rocker studs. A quick check in the Sealed Power catalog showed they offer a +.150-inch-long pushrod, which would solve the interference problem. With the correct pushrods (No. RP3212), the final assembly began.

Degreeing the camshaft showed the Sealed Power large-pin performance timing chain and gear set (No. 2204101) and the Edelbrock cam were completely accurate according to the specification card supplied with the cam. The short-block was assembled and topped off with a Sealed Power high-volume oil pump (No. 224-4143) and pickup screen (No. 224-1246). The oil pump intermediate driveshaft (No. 224-6146E) has a steel collar instead of the usual plastic one found on a replacement shaft. Using Fel-Pro gaskets throughout, the engine was completed by installing the original, factory, aluminum dual-plane high-rise intake manifold and a brand new Holley 780cfm vacuum-secondary carburetor (No. 0-4800-1). The Holley carburetor is one of the new musclecar re-releases, thus duplicating as nearly as possible the original status of the engine.

To upgrade the factory ignition system that consisted of a normal point-type distributor, Jim chose all MSD components from Autotronic Controls. Using a magnetic pickup distributor (No. 8461), alkyd rotor (No. 8462), a vacuum-advance

mechanism (No. 8463), a distributor cap (No. 8437), an 8mm spark plug wire set (No. 3110), a Blaster 2 coil (No. 8203) and a 6A ignition module (No. 6200), the ignition system was prepared for any situation that could possibly be encountered in the street environment. The distributor was set up to have a total of 26 crankshaft degrees by 3200 rpm so that, when combined with an initial advance of 12 degrees, the total centrifugal advance would be 38 degrees.

Jim chose to use Hooker headers (No. 2117). The old headers had rusted badly and he wanted to avoid a repeat situation so when he learned that High Performance Coatings, in Oklahoma City, Oklahoma, offered a coating that could be applied to the inside as well as the outside of the headers and would last indefinitely, he decided to send his new ones there for treatment. The coating also reduces the heat radiation into the engine compartment, thereby reducing carburetor air temperatures and increasing performance.

Running an engine on a dynamometer is the best way to see exactly how efficient and powerful it is. The dyno gives precise readings of air/fuel ratio, the ability of the engine to breathe, the torque output, horsepower, etc. We were able to schedule two days of dyno time at the dynamometer research facility of AirFlow Research in Pacoima, California. AirFlow owns an ultra-modern Superflow 901-C dyno, which makes running the tests a breeze. The LT-1 was bolted up and, after a final check of all the components,

20_All finished and ready to go, the LT-1 waits to prove itself on the dyno at AirFlow Research. This is always nervous time for engine builders, and since this is Jim Redding Jr.'s first performance engine, he's twice as nervous._

SOURCE LIST

AirFlow Research Cylinder Heads and Dyno Facility
10490 Ilex Ave.
Pacoima, CA 91331
(818) 890-0616

B&B Performance Sales
23190 Del Lago Dr.
Laguna Hills, CA 92654
(714) 586-0561

Chaffey College
5885 Haven Ave.
Alta Loma, CA 91701
(714) 822-4484

Edelbrock Equipment Corp.
411 Coral Circle Dr.
El Segundo, CA 90245
(213) 322-7310

Fel-Pro
7540 N. McCormick Blvd.
Skokie, IL 60076
(312) 761-4500

Holley Replacement Parts Division
11955 E. Nine Mile Rd.
Warren, MI 48090

Hooker Headers
1024 W. Brooks St.
Ontario, CA 91762
(714) 983-5871

HPC/High Performance Coatings
1107 Cornell Pkwy.
Oklahoma City, OK 73108
(405) 943-8464

MSD/Autotronic Controls
6908 Commerce
El Paso, TX 79915
(915) 772-7431

Polyrock
4763 Murrieta St.
P.O. Box 886
Chino, CA 91710
(714) 591-4885

Sealed Power Corp.
1854 E. 22nd St.
Los Angeles, CA 90058

21 The MSD distributor performed flawlessly as did the MSD 6A ignition module and coil. The wires are MSD Heli-core, among the best available for performance without causing radio interference.

22 Here's what the HPC-coated Hooker headers looked like after running the tests. This is really some incredible stuff. The plugs at the top of each tube are for the factory A.I.R. fittings which are used when the engine goes into the car.

was fired to life by Guy Tripp, master of the AirFlow dyno controls. The engine was checked for leaks immediately and, none being found, was set for 20 degrees of timing advance at 2000 rpm and run for 45 minutes to give the camshaft a chance to break in thoroughly. Since it's absolutely imperative that the engine not be allowed to idle below 1500 rpm for the first 20 to 45 minutes of life, the 20 degrees at 2000 rpm is a safe advance figure for breaking in the engine.

After the break-in period, we removed the rocker arm covers to check for any metallic particles or water in the oil. Not finding either, we were about to put the covers back on when Jim noticed the rocker arms were just barely touching the cast-in drippers of the factory LT-1 rocker arm covers. A quick trim and we were in business again.

As always when running a new or unknown combination on a dyno, carburetor calibration mustn't be too lean. Running an engine rich on the dyno doesn't hurt anything; running one lean can instantly destroy it. Our fuel checks showed we were rich so we were okay for a first test. The dyno was programmed to run the engine from 2500 to 6000 rpm in 500rpm increments.

The first test confirmed that the carburetor calibration was indeed rich for this engine combination by producing wide-open throttle air/fuel ratios between 8 and 9:1. We changed the jets on the primary side of the carburetor until the air/fuel ratios were closer to the range of 11 and 12:1. We used the torque reading as a verification that we weren't going too lean and consequently losing power. The base test with the rich jetting showed a maximum torque reading of 375 ft.-lbs. at 4000 rpm. After achieving the correct air/fuel ratio we were still showing a maximum torque reading of 375 ft.-lbs., only this time the torque peak shifted up to 4500 rpm.

Satisfied that the carburetor jetting was correct, we ran a test with the total timing at 40 degrees and lost a little power. The timing was then changed to 36 degrees total and again we lost a little power. We returned the timing to the original 38 degrees total and re-ran the test to verify the timing; the engine responded by repeating its earlier best of 375 ft.-lbs. of torque. In 1971, Chevrolet rated the LT-1 at 330 horsepower through the stock exhaust system. With headers, which can sometimes account for quite an increase in horsepower, our maximum horsepower reading was 357 at 5500 rpm, so it may be concluded that the original engine, on a dyno with the addition of a set of headers, could have achieved this figure.

This was Jim's goal—to duplicate the performance of the LT-1 350 of 1971 and be able to drive the car and experience the same thrill as his father. The performance spirit lives on in this Camaro and is showing healthy signs of a long life to come. **C**